SOVIET AND AMERICAN POLICIES
IN THE UNITED NATIONS

SOVIET AND AMERICAN POLICIES IN THE UNITED NATIONS:

A Twenty-Five-Year Perspective

Edited by

Alvin Z. Rubinstein
University of Pennsylvania
AND
George Ginsburgs
Graduate Faculty, New School for Social Research

New York University Press
New York 1971

To Frankie and Ida

INTRODUCTION

The United Nations is twenty-five years old, its proceedings and actions a matter of record, its accomplishments a subject of dispute. To speak of "celebrating" the anniversary would perhaps be inappropriate because the achievements of the past generation have not approximated the expectations of 1945 and because the prospects for the future are less than encouraging. In 1945 hopes were high that the United Nations, led by the five great powers —the permanent members of the Security Council—would preserve the peace, facilitate great-power cooperation, and promote economic development in colonial and underdeveloped areas. Since then the world organization has weathered many crises, international and institutional, and in the process has undergone unforeseen transformations, such as the increased political importance of the General Assembly; the enormous expansion of developmental and welfare functions; and the effect of regional and bloc proclivities upon approaches to concrete problems.

From its very inception the United Nations was transformed by the falling-out and global struggle between the Soviet Union and the United States. Their rivalry has been an essential dimension of the U.N. experience, influencing virtually all spheres of activity. Yet, if the superpowers significantly influenced the United Nations, they, in turn, have not been untouched by interaction with the organization they have so dominated. Thus, the Soviet Union and the United States started by opposing each other and imperiously imposing a bipolarity on U.N. deliberations. The result was an American-dominated U.N. during the first postwar decade: what Washington deemed good for the United States was considered good for the United Nations; Moscow settled for the authority to scuttle any effort by the U.N. to intrude a noncommunist presence into the Soviet empire. By the mid-1950's, the superpower struggle assumed a less perilously military stance. Leaderships changed and mutual possession of nuclear weapons made war between the Soviet Union and the United States unthinkable as a basis for advancing national ambitions and imperial systems. Within the United Nations, decolonization and the appeal of nonalignment generated democratizing pressures for greater involvement in international decision making by the mushrooming membership of small nations; and these tended also to mitigate cold war cleavages. Increasingly the superpowers competed for the favor of the Third World and worked to improve their image abroad. Most recently, in their attempts at conflict management, they have staked out positions which seem, once again, indifferent to the importunities of the less powerful. In their negotiation of agreements regarding the regulation of outer space and nuclear nonproliferation, and in their initiating Strategic Arms Limitation Talks (SALT) in Vienna in mid-April 1970, the superpowers are acting as much on their belief that only they fully understand and are capable of settling the critical and pressing issues of the missile-space age, as on their perception of the United Nations as incapable of participating meaningfully in the negotiation of the main problems which affect the superpowers and, by implication, the entire world community.

To understand the past record, present travail, and future potential of the United Nations, it is essential to examine the interaction of the Soviet Union and the United States in a number of areas of profound and persisting contention during the 1945–1970 period. To this end, on October 30 and 31, 1969, under the aegis of The Rena and Angelius Anspach Institute for Diplomacy and Foreign Affairs of the University of Pennsylvania, a conference was convened in Philadelphia to explore selected aspects of Soviet-American interaction within the framework of the United Nations. In the interests of comparative analysis and the elicitation of meaningful generalizations about the foreign policy and international outlook of the two superpowers in the United Nations, the participants were requested (*a*) to identify the assumptions underlying Soviet and American policies; (*b*) to identify key policy objectives and the extent to which these have been attained or have changed; (*c*) to analyze the domestic and international determinants that shaped the assumptions, policies, and behavior of each superpower; (*d*) to assess the ways in which Soviet and American policies have affected, and in turn been affected by, those of the other, and by the specific demands inhering in participation in the United Nations; and (*e*) to evaluate the impact of superpower behavior on the evolution of the United Nations.

At the conference, six papers were presented; a seventh has been added by the editors. Robert G. Wesson examines a generation of interaction against a background of the cold war, limited détente, and adaptation to a changing international environment; and he shows the linkages between Soviet and American behavior in the U.N. and the belief systems and domestic considerations that shape their respective foreign policy outlooks. Arthur Lall brings his many years of diplomatic experience to bear on an analysis of Soviet and American aims and *modus operandi* in the realm of disarmament. Harold K. Jacobson focuses on decolonization, in terms of its impact on both the superpowers and the U.N. itself. Daniel S. Cheever explores one aspect of the over-all problem of promoting the development of the less developed countries—the regulation of the sea bed, and illustrates the complexity and difficulty of trying to reconcile superpower interests with the needs of the weaker nations. James Patrick Sewell traces the interlocking considerations that compose the peacekeeping complex. Edward McWhinney reveals the long road that is yet to be traversed until law can be utilized to regulate the behavior of the superpowers. The editors offer some observations on the factors most likely to shape the superpower interaction in the future.

Inevitably, a number of important subjects in which the Soviet Union and the United States have been intimately involved are not treated due to limitations of space; for example, the evolution of U.N. economic and technical-assistance activities and institutions; the regulation of outer space; the implementation (or nonimplementation) of the U.N.'s commitment to human rights; social and cultural activities; administrative and financial problems; and the role of regional organizations and regionalism.

It is with pleasure and appreciation that we acknowledge the contributions of the following discussants to the success of the conference: Professor Franz Gross, Penn Morton College; Professor Philip E. Jacob, University of Pennsylvania; Professor Douglas M. Johnston, University of Toronto; Professor Oliver J. Lissitzyn, Columbia University; Professor Noyes Leech and Professor Covey Oliver, University of Pennsylvania; Professor Niger Rodley, New School for Social Research; and Professor Oles Smolansky, Lehigh University. Professor Richard N. Swift of New York University read the manuscript and offered valuable suggestions which helped in the preparation of the final draft.

ALVIN Z. RUBINSTEIN
GEORGE GINSBURGS

Philadelphia

CONTENTS

CONTRIBUTORS

DANIEL S. CHEEVER is Professor of International Affairs and Political Science and Director of the Department of International Affairs at the University of Pittsburgh. He is a frequent contributor to *International Organization,* and was recently a Visiting Research Scholar with the Carnegie Endowment for International Peace.

GEORGE GINSBURGS is Associate Professor and Chairman of the Department of Political Science in the Graduate Faculty, New School for Social Research in New York City. His publications include *Soviet Citizenship Law* and *Communist China and Tibet: The First Dozen Years.*

HAROLD KARAN JACOBSON is Professor of Political Science and Director of the International Organization Program at the University of Michigan. He is author of *The U.S.S.R. and the U.N.'s Economic and Social Activities* and coauthor of *Diplomats, Scientists, and Politicians: The United States and the Nuclear Test Ban Negotiations.*

ARTHUR LALL, former permanent representative of India at the United Nations, is Adjunct Professor of International Affairs at Columbia University. He is the author of *The U.N. and the Middle East Crisis, 1967* and *Modern International Negotiation.*

EDWARD McWHINNEY is Professor of Law and Director of the Institute of Air and Space Law at McGill University.

His publications include *International Law and World Revolution* and *Conflit idéologique et Ordre public mondial.*

ALVIN Z. RUBINSTEIN is Professor of Political Science at the University of Pennsylvania. He is the author of *Yugoslavia and the Nonaligned World* and *The Soviets in International Organization: Changing Policy Toward Developing Countries, 1953–1963.*

JAMES PATRICK SEWELL is Associate Professor of Political Science at Yale University. A frequent contributor to scholarly journals, he is also author of *Functionalism and World Politics.*

ROBERT G. WESSON is Professor of Political Science at the University of California at Santa Barbara. His writings include *Soviet Foreign Policy in Perspective* and *Soviet Communes.*

THE UNITED NATIONS IN THE WORLD OUTLOOK OF THE SOVIET UNION AND OF THE UNITED STATES

Robert G. Wesson

During its quarter century, the United Nations has been dominated by the conflicting policies and interests of the two superpowers, whose mutual toleration is necessary for its viability. Although the world organization has seldom played a major role in the foreign policy of either, nowhere else have they so continually confronted each other. Nowhere else can the differences and similarities of their outlooks be so well measured.

Although the United Nations has evolved into something rather different from what its founders had in mind, and both Soviet and American policies in that body have changed markedly, the changes have been mostly of tactics, while fundamental purposes on both sides have remained much the same from 1945 to 1970. The Soviet Union has never seen more than a limited political utility in the United Nations and has stood against its growth as an international entity. The United States, on the contrary, has laid large and at times excessive hopes on the United Nations as a means to world order while failing to exert corresponding practical efforts toward its strengthening.

These general attitudes are older than the United Nations. In the 1920's the Soviet Union regarded the League of Nations with the most intense distrust, practically as a conspiracy against itself. Dominated by the powers that had led the Allied intervention in the civil war, the League sought to maintain peace and the *status quo*. It was hence the natural enemy of the Bolshevik world revolutionary movement, an agent (in the Comintern view) for the intensification of capitalist enslavement, a "league of bandits" in Lenin's expression. This attitude was somewhat moderated as world revolution lost priority, and the Soviet Union joined some specialized agencies of the League for practical purposes. But only when there arose direct threats to Soviet security from militaristic Japan and National-Socialist Germany was the Soviet Union persuaded that the utility of working in the League outweighed ideological antipathy. The Russians then became the most vocal advocates of collective security through the League and strongly supported its feeble efforts to check fascist aggression. They also found in it their best rostrum for proclamations of good intentions on disarmament and such issues, reaping not a little prestige thereby. After efforts toward collective security had come to naught, however, the Soviet Union was subjected to the most vigorous move the League ever undertook: expulsion, in December 1939, for the attack on Finland. The Soviet Government reverted to its first view, that the League was wholly bad.

On the contrary, the United States was largely responsible, through President Wilson, for the conception and the birth of the League of Nations and had viewed it as the potential basis of a new world order. By accidents of politics and personalities and the difference between executive and legislative views of American responsibilities (a difference that has hampered American relations with the United Nations also), the United States failed to join and make use of the League. Although it tried to cooperate at times against aggressors in Europe and Asia, the United States offered little but advice and qualified moral support. Consequently, when World War II engulfed American neutrality, there was some feeling that the catastrophe might have been avoided if the United States had by its participation given the League strength to resist aggression.

It was with a purpose of atoning for this guilt or making up for this error that the United States, under the leadership of Franklin Roosevelt (as firm an internationalist as Woodrow Wilson), approached the task of converting the wartime alliance

of the United Nations into a peacekeeping body. Of all governments, the American was most concerned to make the United
Nations an instrument of world order. Involving the United
States in world affairs, it should preclude the rebirth of isolation-
ism. It should provide sufficient security that big armies would
be unnecessary and spheres of influence would become obsolete.
It would provide a better guarantee for France than the dismemberment of Germany and for the Soviet Union than a sphere
of influence in Eastern Europe. It should form the framework of
a new world order of freedom, American style, to which the
Soviet Union, by the force of world opinion, would be con-
strained to subscribe. Consequently, at the successive summit
conferences of Teheran, Yalta (especially), and Potsdam, the
United States was sufficiently desirous of securing Soviet consent
to the principle of international organization to make concessions
to the Soviet sphere of influence.

If the chief American objective at Yalta was the creation
of the United Nations, Stalin was concerned with more material
gains, reparations, and control over Poland. He displayed less
interest in the United Nations than in any other major subject
and had not even troubled to familiarize himself with proposals
regarding it.[1] In succeeding months, the Russians were willing
to go along with the Americans in its establishment provided they
received assurances that it would be harmless, but they attributed
to it only marginal importance as at best a secondary guarantee
against a renewal of German aggression, a means of continuing
elements of wartime cooperation, and perhaps a potential restraint upon the United States.

When representatives of forty-five states gathered at San
Francisco to draw up the Charter, Stalin showed but little interest, and Soviet bargaining was directed in all areas toward
limiting the scope and competence of the world organization.
One of the most important questions was definition of the veto
power. All of the principal leaders thought of the peacetime
United Nations somewhat in terms of the wartime coalition,
which could function only on the assumption of collaboration
of the leaders and which could hardly be conceived of as co-
ercing any great power. It was assumed that the Security Council

would have at its disposal military contingents furnished by the great powers, and it was highly unrealistic to assume that they might be called upon to take action contrary to the wishes of their own governments. It was clear in any case that the American Senate could not be expected to ratify the United Nations Charter unless this country had a right of veto. Although agreeing on the principle of great-power unanimity, the Soviet Union and the United States disagreed upon its importance and extent. The former stressed the veto, and has to this day continued to stress it, as the sacrosanct fundamental of the United Nations, and wished it to be permitted even to block discussion in the Security Council of any question objectionable to a permanent member. The Soviets realized, of course, that they were apt usually to be in the minority and so were the more anxious for a veto to protect themselves and incidentally to increase their bargaining power.

The United States, supported by Britain, wished to exclude procedural matters from the veto. Molotov remained adamant and for a time there were fears that the San Francisco conference might fail over this rather minor issue. It was necessary for the Western powers to appeal to Stalin over the head of the Soviet Foreign Minister in order to get Soviet acquiescence to making the veto inapplicable with respect to initiating discussion in the Security Council. In fact, the Soviet Union was to establish the principle of the "double veto," whereby it could veto the classification of an issue as procedural. But the question of great-power veto has probably turned out to be less serious than it at times appeared.[2] It is politically realistic; the U.N. can hardly contemplate actions against the United States or the Soviet Union, and the other permanent members have on occasion seen fit to exercise their right of veto. The "double veto" has been used only three times and not since 1948. The Soviets have cast well over a hundred vetoes, some of them rather frivolous and going far beyond the basic purpose of safeguarding a great power against coercion. Among the first Soviet vetoes were those against resolutions on the Syrian–Lebanese issue and on the Franco regime on the grounds that their language was insufficiently strong. But about half of all

Soviet vetoes were on membership applications, which practically ceased to be controversial after 1955 with the mass admission of new nations. Since 1947 the veto has been softened by the practice of permitting abstention, an alternative invented by the Russians and not contemplated by the Charter. Moreover, ways have been found of circumventing a veto in the Security Council by carrying questions to the General Assembly or, to some extent, calling upon the Secretariat to use its judgment within rather broad guidelines. The latter occurred in the Congo affair.

The United States was wise to set about securing agreement on the world organization while wartime cooperation was still strong and had not yet run into the problem of defining the terms of the peace. However, there were several other major differences besides the veto to be hammered out at San Francisco. One of these was the extent to which power should be shared outside the very narrow circle of true great powers. The Soviet Union thought in terms of a diarchy. Stalin was always thoroughly aware of the hard facts of power, particularly military power, and he was quite frank, as Khrushchev was later, in refusing to submit the Soviet Union to the judgment of the smaller powers. In the Soviet view, the equal sovereignty of all members and their authority in the Assembly should be somewhat like the sovereign equality of Soviet republics—more form than substance, a concession to appearances not allowed to interfere with the central directorate's power of decision. Stalin wanted sixteen Assembly places, one for each Soviet republic, and settled for three; and he was perfectly willing for the United States to have an equal number. He was unenthusiastic, however, about the place of militarily weak France and China, and would have preferred to make the Assembly little more than window dressing. The United States wanted a broader governing board, including defeated France and a China whose status rested only on hopes and population figures. Like the Russians, the Americans did not at first contemplate giving much authority to the Assembly. But the implications of a cynical deal were enough to cause the United States to renounce the extra seats, and when the smaller powers clamored at San Francisco for a greater share of authority, to concede enough so that the Assembly achieved authority in practice probably superior to that of the Security Council. For a time, of course, this was advantageous to the United States, whose Latin American and European friends dominated the Assembly in the first years. Ultimately, it became rather advantageous to the Soviet Union, as the Assembly was overwhelmed by new nations of antiwestern disposition and provided the best of forums for antiwestern oratory.

Another and parallel clash of Soviet and American views came over the scope of the United Nations' work. The Soviet interest in the League of Nations had been entirely in its hoped-for contribution to Soviet security, and the same was desired of the United Nations—that it serve only as a barrier to aggression. The Soviets even argued at Dumbarton Oaks that the multiplicity of functions of the League was a reason for its failure. The United States took the position (ironically, more in harmony with Marxism-Leninism) that the causes of war were at least in part economic; hence a world organization should contribute to the alleviation of economic and social tensions by attacking ignorance, poverty, and backwardness. The American view prevailed, and the United Nations was endowed with economic and social as well as security functions. The Soviet Union exercised its privilege of largely ignoring them. Molotov's speech at the founding conference made no reference to the ameliorative purposes, and Soviet references to the United Nations to this day have ordinarily mentioned only the political activities.

Cold War and Stalinism

American favor for world organization was reinforced by the fact that in East-West disputes the United States could count on a majority of 45 or 50 to 5 or 6, the three Soviet delegations being able to count only on Poland and Yugoslavia (until the break in 1948), or Czechoslovakia (after the 1948 coup). It was easy in this situation for the American Government to propose that the United Nations handle almost any international problem. For example, when Stalin repeatedly brought out demands for control of the Straits, James Byrnes repeatedly countered that the United Nations should be made responsible for freedom of navigation.[3] The problem of refugees who did not wish to return to their Soviet homeland was entrusted to a United Nations control of Japanese islands was legitimized by United Nations trusteeship. In 1945–1946, the Security Council helped exert organization, to the grave displeasure of the Russians. American pressure on the Russians to withdraw their forces from Iran, where they were remaining after the agreed deadline and promoting a separatist regime. In response, the Soviet delegate staged his first walkout; nevertheless, the outcome of the case was successful—Soviet forces pulled out without real compensation. This encouraged the United States to look to the United Nations as a court to resolve any differences, such as the Austrian peace settlement, which could not be settled by direct negotiations, as well as deal with such new problems as the danger of an atomic arms race.

The predictable Soviet reaction was a propagandistic counterattack. The response to the inclusion of the Iranian case on the Security Council agenda was a Soviet assault on the British role in Greece, which had previously been accepted quite calmly. As the communist-led insurrection in Greece gained force, the United States, proclaiming the Truman Doctrine, stepped in to check it and was considerably assisted in the process by the U.N. Balkan Commission, which reported communist infiltration and supply from outside. Soviet fury in and against the United Nations mounted higher. Only in a few cases, where the United Nations visibly contributed to the decrease of Western influence, as in hastening the departure of British and French forces from Syria and Lebanon and of Netherlands forces from the Indies could the Russians see any good in it. The Soviets joined in support of the independence of Israel in order further to weaken the British empire. But soon the Soviet view of the U.N. and all its works became almost totally negative and remained so down to the end of Stalin's reign.

One reason for negativism was the fading hope of coming to acceptable agreements with the Western powers. Negotiations both outside the U.N. framework and within it—on Germany and Austria, on economic collaboration (the Soviet rejection of the Marshall Plan being imposed on the satellites), on the control of atomic energy (the Baruch Plan, wrecked because of Soviet insistence on and American refusal to countenance the veto over controls), and on the establishment of a U.N. security force as called for in the Charter—were all frustrated, despite endless and irritating discussions. Another reason was sensitivity regarding the Soviet sphere in East Europe, Western or U.N. interest in which appeared as a direct threat. Concurrently, within the Soviet Union, the limited relaxation of the war years gave way to intensified Stalinism, xenophobia, repression, and doctrinaire anti-westernism. Inevitably, the United Nations, dominated by Western, noncommunist powers, and strongly influenced by the United States, was seen as a class enemy and a wholly evil affair.

Soviet policy became little more, as the Soviets put it, than preventing the United Nations from being made an instrument of imperialism and using it to check the warmongers, or, as the West saw it, than obstructionism and propaganda. Stalinist nar-Nations; the Soviet Union was a member only of the specialized rowness had little appreciation of any positive utility in the United agencies of the most obvious practical value, such as those charged with postal, telecommunications, and meteorological questions; it withdrew from the World Health Organization. Nonparticipation in other programs, even those favored by neutralist powers, was justified on grounds of national sovereignty and by reasoning that they would be capitalist-dominated and so inimical in any case. Through the entire Stalin period there were no Soviet experts at all in United Nations technical assistance programs.[4] Hostility was especially intense toward the United Nations trade and financial agencies, which were seen as promoting a multilateral trading system useful only to the West. Bilateralism, the Soviet claimed, was the way to protect sovereignty and equality of states.[5]

Almost the only positive utility the Russians saw in the United Nations was as a rostrum from which to shout their message to the world. They sought to promote and identify themselves with various virtuous causes, such as opposition to the Franco government, to South African racial policies, and to colonial empires and the manner of their liquidation.[6] They made much of supposed inherent ailments of capitalism, such as prostitution and unemployment, demanding investigations and condemnation despite some disharmony with general insistence on national sovereignty and domestic jurisdiction. They made superficially attractive proposals for disarmament with little consideration for their practicality and no provision for verification but simple trust in the good faith, *inter alios,* of Stalinist Russia. They denounced Western assistance to less developed countries as neocolonialism and contended that loans and credits to them should be extended through the United Nations only. They damned private investment in the Third World as exploitation if not enslavement, at the same time refusing to participate in the drafting of a Code for International Investment on grounds that gradualism and piecemeal reform were useless.

The Soviet campaign was successful enough, despite the large pro-Western majority, that the United States moved away from reliance on the United Nations as an instrument for building the postwar order. The Russians having rejected the Marshall Plan, the United States was disinclined to extend economic aid in a U.N. framework subject to Soviet obstruction. It was also hostile to the establishment of the Special United Nations Fund for Economic Development; the U.N. having proved incapable of opposing communism effectively, the United States would disburse aid with its own untied hands. With the rejection of the Baruch Plan for turning over nuclear production and weapons to an international agency (a scheme that Americans thought very generous but which the Russians deprecated as disguised American domination), the United States largely gave up the idea of atomic disarmament under U.N. auspices, and the desultory negotiations turned into propaganda exercises. By the beginning of 1947, hopes for acting through the U.N. as a means of security were much reduced, and the Truman Doctrine for the defense of Greece and Turkey was propounded without relevance to the international security organization. It was useful to have the reports of the U.N. Balkan Commission, but this was of marginal importance. The United States sought its own solution to the Berlin blockade, and created its own security agency in the North

Atlantic Treaty Organization. In the first part of 1950, the United States even found itself strongly at odds with the U.N. Secretary-General, Trygve Lie, because of his advocacy of the Peking government's claim to the representation of China. The same issue, oddly enough, alienated the Soviet Union still more, as Soviet representatives withdrew from the Security Council and other U.N. bodies only to return more than six months later under the pressure of the Korean war.

The Korean War shelved the Chinese representation issue for the time being. It also had important and contradictory effects on American and Soviet policies regarding the United Nations. During the Korean conflict, the United Nations seemed more useful to the United States than it had been previously. It was extremely helpful that a U.N. commission was on hand to certify the facts of communist aggression and to give the lie, with international authority, to Soviet allegations of an attack by the Republic of Korea. The authorization for intervention, given by the Security Council in the absence of the Soviet delegate, did much to make the largely American military action acceptable to the American public and the world at large. When the Soviet delegate resumed his place in August 1950, international feelings against the unprovoked Communist attack on S. Korea and subsequent Russian attempts to shield the guilty parties through obstructionist tactics in the Security Council were running high enough that the United States was able to secure the adoption, by a vote of 52 to 5 with two abstentions, of the "Uniting for Peace" resolution, stretching the Charter to give the General Assembly a role in peacekeeping in default of the Security Council. When the term of office of Trygve Lie expired and the Russians sought, because of his vigorous support for the U.N. role in Korea, to prevent his reelection, he was continued in office at American insistence for this very reason, so that the Russians would not be able to punish him for his stand. On the other hand, the United States had to conclude from the Korean experiment that the U.N. added little to American security. As a peacekeeping operation, it was not a success, and as the war progressed U.N. support for American purposes—enlarged to the reunification of Korea under the U.N. aegis—diminished. Failure to achieve victory reduced U.N. prestige, and a number of neutrals, led by India, began backing away from the Western side.

The continuation of Lie in office by action of the Assembly after the Soviets blocked his reelection in the Security Council stands in marked contrast with the latter day practice based on the assumption that the Secretary General must be fully acceptable to East as well as West, and the incident showed how isolated and impotent the Soviet Union had become in the U.N. Soviet frustration and dislike for the U.N. were greatly increased by its position in the Korean conflict. Yet that crisis helped to set in motion a turn of Soviet policy toward greater involvement in and utilization of the world organization. The Soviets learned from their miscalculation in staying out of the crucial Security Council meeting on Korea; since then, no Soviet representative has ever walked out of any U.N. organization. The Soviet Government also observed that many leaders of the less developed countries supported American policy in Korea only halfheartedly or not at all and that they might usefully be cultivated. Previously the Soviet Government had contended that independence peacefully acquired could not be real and "bourgeois" governments of excolonial countries must be stooges, and it had often offended them by treating them as such while encouraging revolution against them. Despite such treatment, there had been some warmth in the less developed countries toward the Soviet Union, partly because of admiration for its independent industrialization, partly because of sensitivity to their dependence on the West. After 1950, the Soviet Union began, at first hesitantly and on a small scale, but with increasing emphasis and purpose for a decade, to take advantage of these facts in the United Nations and out of it.

Competitive Coexistence

The failure because of the Korean War of Stalin's last attempt at expansion was only one of several obvious causes for the strategic change of Soviet foreign policy in the years prior to 1956. The disappearance of his forceful personality was an important factor. He had once remarked that without himself his successors would be like "blind kittens," but they had a more sensible perception of the world than he and began shortly after his death to moderate the abrasive aspects of Soviet foreign policy and reduce the isolation into which Stalin had unnecessarily thrust his empire. The situation was ripe for change, moreover. The Soviet Union had done a good deal to overcome the nuclear inferiority of the first postwar years and no longer felt so sensitively defensive toward the world. The Soviet sphere of Eastern Europe had been consolidated and fears of Western influence were moderated. The Soviet economy had made steady and rapid progress, so that it was acceptable on the one hand to open up a little to foreign view and on the other to expend something in the cultivation of Soviet prestige abroad. Hence, after Stalin's death and particularly after Khrushchev won out over his rivals at the beginning of 1955, the Soviet Union was prepared to look to ideological or political expansion in the only inviting area, the Third World.

This required ideological revision and turning away from Stalin's concept of two hostile worlds, the "socialist" and "capitalist" camps, with no neutral or middle ground. Stalin's view was fairly consonant with traditional Marxism-Leninism and the view of history as ruled by class conflict, but it was patently unrealistic in the 1950's and harmful to Soviet prestige. Khrushchev, who wished to rule more by the Communist party and less by police and terror, brought ideology up to date in numerous related ways. In the nuclear era, he conceded that war was no longer to be held inevitable, thereby theoretically opening possibilities of disarmament. He allowed that "socialism" did not have to come by revolution but might emerge by peaceful process; and he held that the neutralist countries, being opposed to imperialism, were at least potential friends of the Soviet Union. Logically, he began a campaign to win over these countries by high-powered salesmanship, economic and military relations, and aid—a campaign which, beginning in India and Egypt but rapidly spreading to many countries, caused the West much apprehension, especially in the years from 1955 to 1961.

This Soviet campaign to convert the Third World was conducted mostly outside the United Nations on a strictly bilateral basis, but it also found the United Nations an important adjunct. This was partly because of the Soviet change of outlook; Khrushchev, unlike Stalin, found the gradualism and ameliorative approach of the world body admissible, and he was encouraged by the change in the composition of the United Nations in 1955 and afterwards. Only nine states joined the U.N. in its first decade, as the United States and the Soviet Union had each blackballed the friends of the other. But in 1955, as a result of the improvement of the international atmosphere, it was agreed to admit nearly all pending candidates together. This practically settled the principle of universality of membership. More and more of the colonial territories, which were rapidly achieving independence, were welcomed in following years, eventually more than doubling the U.N.'s membership. The result of this influx of new nations, many or most of them with grievances against the West and problems and aspirations often closer to those of the Soviet Union than to those of the United States, was to make the world body much more congenial for the former and less satisfactory for the latter.

The Soviet Union continued to utilize the United Nations above all as a sounding board and forum for propaganda, but it did so with a new purposefulness and sophistication. It had considerable success in identifying itself with the aspirations of the less developed countries and in discrediting Western-oriented programs. Former colonies, sensitive and insecure in their new sovereignty, were appreciative of Soviet emphasis on the sacred rights of sovereignty, especially when they were threatened by economic if not political domination by the United States. The Soviets continually warned them to beware of recolonization; and, because of their experience, they were much more apprehensive of Western than communist imperialism. Without trouble or expense to themselves, the Russians could demand that priority be given to heavy industry, which the less developed countries were apt to desire for power and prestige, and decry as hypocritical and selfish Western contentions that this approach was uneconomic. Vehement Soviet boosting of state over private ownership was also popular with many states lacking native capital.

When the Special United Nations Fund for Economic Development (SUNFED) was proposed in 1951 the Soviets opposed it (as did the Americans), supposedly because of lack of sympathy for any developmental program under U.N. auspices; after Stalin's death, they shifted to full support to curry favor with the neutralists and embarrass the West. They proposed extreme measures favored by the less developed countries with little concern for the responsibility of carrying them out; and one may guess, with Rubinstein, that they did not mind if superficially attractive programs were defeated by Western opposition.[7] For example, they were quite free to support resolutions calling for the immediate independence of all non-self-governing territories without regard for circumstances, as the United States could not. They could urge trade concessions to the less developed countries with no obligation of making any concessions in their own controlled foreign exchange. They could demand that the U.N. do more to assist the needier nations without assuming any important amount of the burden, at the same time denouncing "capitalist" countries for using U.N. aid as a means of neocolonialism.[8]

The Soviets did, however, begin using various programs of the U.N. on a limited scale as a means of influence, if not neocolonialism. They joined (or rejoined in the case of WHO) most of the U.N. specialized agencies. Especially significant was the surprise offer, a few months after Stalin died, of a modest four million nonconvertible rubles for the Expanded Program of Technical Assistance (EPTA). Nonconvertibility, generally imposed on Soviet contributions to economic and social agencies of the U.N., meant that expenditures could be controlled in detail by the Soviet Government. At the same time, the Soviet Union wanted its funds spent rather for technicians than for equipment, presumably because the former could be more politically effective. Soviet technicians on U.N. programs were ordinarily kept as agents of the Soviet Union under surveillance of the embassy and not permitted to become international civil servants.

The purpose of Soviet contributions to U.N. programs being to gain entry to them and to reduce their utility to the West, Soviet participation was strictly limited. For many months, there were no takers for the original offer of four million rubles, partly because of distrust, partly because of bureaucratic clumsiness and the limitations on its use. Gradually, however, a few Soviet experts found their way to less developed countries, first and principally India, which alone received 60 per cent of Soviet aid furnished through the U.N. from 1955 to 1962.[9] Yet even there, the bilateral Soviet program involved over twenty times as many experts. By 1963, when Soviet participation in U.N. programs had reached its height, 160 Soviet experts were reported to be engaged in various countries.[10] Regularly the Soviet Union would complain of the growth of specialized agencies and try to reduce their budgets or at least to block their expansion.[11] The Soviet Union has always insisted on the voluntary nature of contributions to economic and social agencies, making this practically a sacred principle. Only a very small fraction of Soviet foreign aid (as was true also of American) was channeled through the U.N. Khrushchev, like Molotov fifteen years earlier, neglected to mention this side of the U.N.'s work in his address before that body in 1960.

Soviet participation in the Suez crisis of 1956 was very much in the same spirit. Maximum propagandistic use was made of the affair both within the U.N. and outside it, with denunciation of imperialism, vague threats of rocket reprisals, and offers (made when the need had passed) to send volunteers to help Egypt. Yet even when the U.N. was performing a function of which the Soviet Union thoroughly approved, such as securing the removal of British, French, and Israeli forces from the Suez area, the Russians declined to give material support. Although they favored the employment of the United Nations Emergency Force (UNEF), they refused to pay any part of its cost, with the perhaps attractive but politically unrealistic argument that Britain, France, and Israel should pay all the expenses of the action directed against themselves.

The Suez crisis, coupled with the Soviet repression of the Hungarian rebellion, also showed the changed character of the United Nations. Quite contrary to the original image of the U.N., as an agency for joint peacekeeping by the great powers, the superpowers did not participate directly in UNEF, contingents for which were drawn from small neutrals. The best function of the U.N. was precisely to keep the superpowers disengaged.[12]

The episode also showed that the majority of the U.N. members were much less concerned with oppression of Europeans than of Arabs. A resolution of the General Assembly called for withdrawal of Soviet troops from Hungary and an investigation by the Secretary-General, but there was no proposal for military action or indeed for any milder sanctions. When the Soviets scornfully disregarded the Assembly, the matter was shelved without much protest.

Because of such attitudes and the divergence of the interests of a majority of the members of the U. N. from those which most concerned the United States, there was a widespread feeling in the United States in the latter 1950's that the world organization was Communist-dominated. American policy in the U.N. was also pulled in opposite directions by conflicting demands of NATO partners versus the desire to please ex-colonial countries, by commitment to the principles of legality and stability versus the urge for change. For example, the United States felt obliged to condemn the Indian overrunning of Goa, to the dismay of many of the Third World and the political profit of the Soviet Union. For such reasons, American support for the U.N. declined.

Peacekeeping Controversy

In the Congo crisis of 1960–1964 the peacekeeping function of the U.N. scored its greatest success to date. A substantial army of international composition, unlike the almost wholly American U.N. force in Korea, restored order in a troubled country and ended the secession of its wealthiest province. Yet the prolonged and tangled affair ironically resulted in a grave weakening of the organization and severe curtailment of its capacity to act against any future threat to peace.

When the United Nations first entered the Congo to replace Belgian forces hastily sent to protect Europeans, the United States and the Soviet Union were in full agreement. Soon, however, they differed, as the question of what kind of government the Congo should have came to the fore. The Soviet Union, then near the height of its hopes for influencing the development of emerging nations, wanted the U.N. to remove the Belgians and then let local radical elements encouraged by itself take over the government. The United States wished the U.N. to promote stability and moderation. The United States was able to secure this though not through the Security Council, immobilized by the veto, nor through the General Assembly, which was divided and uncertain in its purposes, but through the Secretariat, charged with carrying out broad resolutions of the other organs. It would hardly be an exaggeration to say that the Secretariat carried out American policies for several years, and where the Russians had once seen a magnificent opportunity for the installation of a revolutionary, anti-Western if not procommunist, regime, there eventually emerged under American and U.N. guidance a pro-Western and anti-Soviet government.

Soviet leaders, although refraining from dangerous commitments, reacted with verbal violence. They went so far as to accuse Secretary-General Hammarskjöld of complicity in the murder of former Congolese Premier Patrice Lumumba, and Khrushchev showed his contempt for the U.N. by his manners, including shoe-banging and shouts from the floor, when he participated in the 1960 General Assembly. The Soviet Union particularly protested the Secretary-General's role. It was far from their wishes that he should emerge as something of an independent international force (although in the Iranian case they had been glad to give a broad interpretation to his powers, contrary to American desires [13]). It was a natural evolution that the administrative center should acquire more power of decision as the organization grew and as the legally decisive bodies failed to act effectively because of their divisions, but it was contrary to both Soviet policy and philosophy when Hammarskjöld spoke of his right "to express what may be called the independent judgment of the organization." [14] If the Soviets were to countenance a U.N. military force, it could only be under the close and detailed control of the veto-bound Security Council.

The Russians sought to reorganize the United Nations administration and to check its activity by what amounted to a financial veto—refusal to pay any share of the operations of which they disapproved. Until Khrushchev dramatically demanded that the Secretariat be made into a tripleheaded "troika," able to move only by agreement of "capitalist," "socialist," and "neutralist" components, the Soviet Union had not paid a great deal of attention to the composition of the Secretariat. There had always been Soviet citizens among the immediate assistants of the Secretary-General, but the United Nations began with a disproportionate percentage of Americans on its staff (partly because of location and convenience) while the Soviet Union furnished very few—in the first decade only about 10 per cent of the number to which it was entitled by its share of the U.N. budget.[15] The main reason seems to have been indifference; Stalin once declined to send more Russians on the truthful grounds that few were qualified,[16] and there was no pressure to make more positions available for Soviet citizens. This neglect of obvious possibilities of influence—or fear of exposure of Russians to the bourgeois world—diminished after the death of Stalin. After 1955, the Soviet Union began complaining of underrepresentation, but it did little to make qualified candidates available, and its share of the U.N. staff has risen very slowly.

The Secretary-General seems to have made considerable effort to meet the charges of discrimination against nationals of the Soviet Union, and other "socialist" states, but there were real problems in securing better geographic distribution. There was no possibility of simply recruiting talent within the Soviet Union, even giving the Soviet government a right of clearance (as the American government was given). Soviet personnel detailed to the United Nations were usually employees of the Foreign Ministry and instead of acting as U.N. staff were often hardly distinguishable from the Soviet delegation. They ordinarily remained only about two years and had neither opportunity nor incentive to become international civil servants; they were less influential than they might have been, even in their small numbers, because of inexperience and isolation. The very idea of impartial international officials is alien to the Soviet scheme, and at one time the Soviets sought to end the Secretariat's practice of hiring on permanent contracts.[17]

It was consequently quite in line with previous Soviet policy when Khrushchev, having taken angry note of the influence of the

Secretariat in the Congo, demanded that it be made representative not of the world organization but of the main political groupings. The impossibility of neutrality was an old idea which the Soviets had only occasionally laid aside; Khrushchev revived it in full force. Beyond his insistence on three Secretaries-General each with veto powers, he proposed that the principle of the troika be applied to the whole staff of the secretariat, to the command structure of any U.N. forces, and indeed to all main U.N. organs.[18] The idea was coldly received even by anti-Western neutralists, as they felt they had a stake in the United Nations and readily perceived that the troika idea would paralyze the organization. The Soviet Union was vehement in its advocacy, however, until the death in 1961 of Secretary-General Hammarskjöld and his replacement by U Thant, who was a reasonable facsimile of the neutral man who Khrushchev averred could not exist—if he did not in fact lean a little more toward East than West.

If Soviet determination to change the Secretariat may have had something to do with the selection of a Secretary-General satisfactory to the "socialist camp," the obdurate Soviet refusal to contribute to the costs of the Congo and other peacekeeping operations was even more successful in curtailing U.N. activities. It meant that henceforward the U.N. had to give up hope of mounting any such venture except on the basis of voluntary contributions.

Claiming that the Congo operations were illegal because they were not duly authorized by the Security Council, the Soviet Union refused to pay any part of its assessment. Gaullist France, unhappy over the U.N. role in the Congo, also refused to contribute anything, as did a number of other nations, the members of the "socialist camp" on principle and the balance pleading poverty. United Nations finances soon became straitened. Although the United States carried about half of the burden, it was necessary to have recourse to a bond issue to cover costs in 1962–1963. The American Congress authorized subscription only by a narrow margin. When the Assembly met in 1964, the United States was determined that failure to pay peacekeeping assessments should be treated like default on regular quotas, that is, that the delinquent nations should be penalized by loss of their vote under Article 19 of the Charter. This position was legally well-founded, (and indeed was supported, in a 9 to 5 advisory opinion, by the International Court of Justice), but it was politically unsound. Since the Soviet Union was determined not to yield, it was unrealistic to expect that Moscow could be made to pay for actions entirely contrary to its desires, especially as the Soviet position was strengthened by the fact that no less than seventeen other nations were in the same situation.

The United States consequently was unable to muster much support for its position that the U.N., practically speaking, had the right to tax its members whether they liked it or not. For a time the General Assembly tried to avoid the issue by avoiding votes—acting only by acclamation, as in the choice of a president —while a solution was sought. The U.N.'s very existence seemed threatened, and it was a melancholy indication of the stature of the world organization that this could come about over a deficit, at the beginning of December 1964, of $111.6 million, a trifling sum compared to arms budgets of major powers. After much wrangling, the United States acknowledged defeat, opting for a weakened U.N. instead of risking destruction of the organization. Thereafter the United States reserved its own right not to pay for operations of which it disapproved thus practically accepting the Soviet version of the powers of the United Nations. The Soviet Union vaguely promised a "voluntary contribution" to help meet the deficit but never made it. In April 1967, the Soviet delegate declined again to specify the time or amount of the "voluntary contribution" and accused the United States of responsibility for the financial troubles of the U.N.[19] By the middle of 1964, the U.N. forces were withdrawn from a tolerably pacified Congo, and later peacekeeping operations, as in Yemen and Cyprus, had to rely on voluntary contributions.

American hopes for the U.N. were also diminished by the continuing influx of excolonial states, mostly small, who found the world forum the most suitable place to make themselves heard. Their position was further improved by enlargement of the Security Council and the Economic and Social Council at the end of 1963. Their passionate concerns, such as the minority government of Rhodesia and South African apartheid, were of secondary importance for the United States; and this country sometimes found itself in a minority, as when the Assembly voted an oil embargo against South Africa in 1963. Contrary to American but in accordance with Soviet wishes, a United Nations Conference on Trade and Development (UNCTAD) was convened in 1964 and made a permanent institution. In it, the less developed nations pressed for such favors as tariff preferences, price supports, and guaranteed markets, which the United States generally frowned upon but which did not embarrass Soviet trading agencies. The United Nations seemed unable, on the other hand, to come to grips with the conflict in Vietnam, and the United States refrained from trying to involve it for a decade until 1965, when it began to seem that anything the United Nations might be able to arrange would be an improvement. The communist side, however, had no wish to bring in the United Nations, and the world body showed complete helplessness in a major threat to world peace. In the Dominican crisis also the United States steered the issue away from the Security Council, which again showed little desire to become involved.

The State Department felt that the United Nations had become less responsible with the addition of many small, weak states which voted freely for actions that others, especially the United States, would be charged with carrying out. Afro-Asian states came to have a majority, so that two thirds of the membership contributed only about 5 per cent of the budget. Because of this disparity of voting power and responsibility, Secretary of State Rusk expressed fears of the "swirling majorities," [20] which lightly passed extreme resolutions, often representing little more than strong hopes. There was discussion of weighted voting, but the United States made no concrete proposals.

After the Cold War

In 1965, the U.N. emerged weakened from its financial crisis, found itself under attack by Gaullist France and some Asian powers, suffered its first withdrawal (Indonesia), and watched helplessly the escalation of war in Vietnam. The Afro-Asians concentrated on such noncentral world issues as the Portuguese colonies and the termination of the South African mandate over South-West Africa. Pressure grew for the liquidation of the remnants of the European colonial empires, and in 1966 a call went out, over American opposition, for help to movements fighting colonialism. In economic questions, the Soviet Union found itself to some extent bracketed with the United States as an advanced industrial country against the less developed countries; a North–South division cut across the old East–West lines.

As the lines of bipolar cleavage became blurred after 1962 and the Afro-Asian majority was not much interested in the issue of communism, the cold war was largely sidetracked. The Soviet Union sought to capitalize on American embarrassment in Vietnam and the landing of marines in the Dominican Republic but without great success, as debates on "intervention" turned also to Eastern Europe and Tibet. The Korean question continued to be rehashed every year. On the other hand, the United States took the initiative in removing the Hungarian issue from the agenda, Soviet support for the admission of Communist China became perfunctory, and the election of a Rumanian as Assembly president in 1967 showed how far the cold war had moved into the background.

The invasion of Czechoslovakia in August 1968 meant only a moderate revival of cold war themes. The Soviet action was denounced in the Security Council and defended by the Soviet delegate, who stated that Soviet forces had entered at the request of the Czechoslovak Government and would be withdrawn as soon as no longer needed for its defense. The United States seemed practically to recognize the Soviet sphere in Eastern Europe, and its indictment of the U.S.S.R. was weakened by its own past position on regional security taken in the Guatemalan and Dominican affairs. The draft resolution on Czechoslovakia, killed by a Russian veto, expressed grave concern over the violation of United Nations principles, called for prompt withdrawal of all foreign troops from the country, and urged members to exercise such influence as they could to secure Soviet compliance, but there was no request for sanctions or suggestion of any kind of coercion, and no move was made to secure action by the General Assembly. The U.N. seemed satisfied to accept the assurances of the new Czech delegation that Soviet troops would presently depart under the August 26 agreement and that it wished the item removed from the agenda. In October 1968, Gromyko in addressing the Assembly bothered only very briefly to discuss the case.

Under the circumstances, the United Nations retained some utility for the superpowers. It continued as always to be a locus for disarmament negotiations, but these made no more progress than during many years of sterile discussions, and between 1968 and 1970 the United States and the Soviet Union moved toward talks on strategic weaponry entirely without reference to the U.N. It was a small plus for the U.N. that under its auspices some agreements were reached on the uses of outer space. However, one of the Soviet reasons for interest in the U.N., the desire to use it to support the Soviet campaign in the Third World, tended to fade. Lacking Khrushchev's optimism, his successors paid less attention to distant lands, concentrating instead on those in the Soviet neighborhood. Soviet bloc developmental aid, far from rising in step with the national incomes in the community, shrank slightly. Many excolonial countries seemed to be turning away from extremes of anti-Westernism, as memories of Western domination receded and they became more aware of economic needs that the communist bloc could not fill.

The chief thrust of Soviet propaganda continued to be in the colonial issue. Soviet delegates in April 1969, for example, berated the United States for colonialism in the Virgin Islands and Guam; and in June they denounced the U.S. and Britain for trading with Rhodesia. But pleasing the less developed countries was not given high priority by the Soviets. At the 1966 Solidarity Conference in Havana the Soviet delegate refused to brand the U.N. as colonialist. To the grave displeasure of the Afro-Asians, the Soviet Union at the end of 1968 sided with the United States in upholding the right of South Africa to participate in a U.N. conference, as it was entitled to do according to the Charter. Not long after, the Russians showed that their European political interests much outweighed any considerations of the U.N. aid program; they threatened to boycott the planning commission for the Second

Development Decade if West Germany were included, although in 1968 the Germans had contributed eight times as much to eight U.N. programs and agencies for development as all the Soviet bloc countries together, $58 million against $7 million.[21] The Soviet Union also supported the United States in warning the smaller powers against budgetary increases which would fall largely on the wealthier countries. When Gromyko made a long and relatively conciliatory statement on foreign policy in July 1969, he did not find it necessary to touch upon the United Nations at all.

American support for the U.N. has also seemed to be qualified.[22] Failure in 1965 and 1966 to obtain U.N. assistance in settling the Vietnam conflict had been disappointing, and U Thant's unsympathetic position on the Vietnam issue was decidedly irritating to the United States. The incapacity of the U.N. to keep the truce in the Near East after the June (1967) war, itself facilitated by the hasty pull-out of the U.N., was also a blow to hopes that the world body could do much directly for international security. There has been some effort to stress the nonpolitical aspects of the U.N. to compensate for its political weaknesses, although the United States has tended to restrict its cooperation with international capital-providing agencies because of balance-of-payments difficulties, and the State Department has seemed uncertain how far it should go in endeavoring to meet demands of the less developed nations for special protection in international trade. If questions of peacekeeping have seemed insoluble, however, the United Nations could nonetheless be valuable in important ways: in control of the drug traffic, management of water resources, promotion of education, regulating the uses of space (including demilitarization and satellite broadcasts), dealing with the population problem, etc.[23]

This shift of emphasis corresponded to the apparent evolution of the United Nations. The world organization grew from 2,500 employees on a budget of $24.7 million in 1946 to 30,000 employees spending $686 million in 1968, and it was definitely a going and growing concern. But its role as guardian of world order seemed to recede, checked by its constitutional limitations, while its role as international coordinator and developer continued to expand, propelled by the needs of the sovereign nations in an increasingly interdependent world. Particularly in the later years, the United Nations has moved from political matters to such items as the exploitation of maritime resources, the control of technology, technical assistance, development surveys, and economic planning; nine-tenths of its manpower is engaged in social and economic work. Despite the passions of the majority of its members, the U.N. has not been able to coerce even minor powers, such as Rhodesia, South Africa, and Portugal, when the big powers did not see their own interests strongly involved. Complying with the wishes of the African states, the U.N. made no attempt to intervene in the Nigerian civil war. But the need for a world organization has grown ever greater, and it has seemed that world community, politically frustrated, might grow on economic necessity.

THE UNITED NATIONS AND SOVIET PURPOSES

Every ambitious nation is ambivalent in its outlook, seeking on the one hand the advantages of peaceful and cooperative relations and on the other hand to better itself competitively, securing objectives such as prestige, commercial privileges, or territorial expansion which are obtainable only at the expense of other states. This dualism is especially strong in the Soviet Union, which is more than a simple national state. In relations with the outside world, the Russians seek the benefits of normal international relations but also maintain doctrinaire hostility to other forms of society and uphold, at least in theory, a mission of imposing their own political order. Not only, in other words, does the Soviet Union behave like a state dealing with other states as equals; it has also the pretensions of a universal polity for which other polities lack real legitimacy and are eventually (with or without revolutionary violence) to be replaced. These two aspects of the Soviet view of the outside world vary in intensity in accordance with internal and external circumstances, but both have at all times been evident in the Soviet approach to the United Nations, to be used both as a means of cooperating with the nonsocialist world and as a means of struggle against it.

The original Soviet purpose in joining the United Nations

may have been entirely the former, mostly, and primarily for security reasons, to maintain a degree of cooperation with wartime allies. At the same time, the Soviet Union had been a member of international technical organizations since long before joining the League of Nations and had every reason to continue as these became affiliated with the new United Nations. Soviet participation in them has never been in question even in the darkest days of Stalinism, as has been noted. It now seems wholly probable that the Soviet Union, drawn like other states more closely into the and other external foreign interests, must find increasing practical international nexus and vigorously expanding maritime, aviation, utility in U.N. agencies. It is even possible that Soviet commercial interests may one day suffice to overcome ideologically based repugnance to U.N. trade and financial agencies. In 1968, Soviet trade with the West amounted to $4.12 billion, an increase of 14 per cent over 1967, while trade with bloc countries grew only 10 per cent.[24]

The U.N. has never functioned as anything like the intended great power directorate, but its conflict-controlling or -resolving functions have nonetheless been valuable for the Soviet Union as for other powers. It has been a useful meeting place for discussions regarding such dangerous matters as the Berlin blockade of 1948 and the settlement of the Korean War. Countless meetings between American and Soviet diplomats have taken place in and around the United Nations headquarters, a valuable supplement to ordinary diplomatic channels. The United Nations has also helped to check many conflicts which the Soviet Union, like other powers, wished to see limited, although the Russians have been very reluctant to see the U.N. wield force.[25] For example, the U.N. role in the Indo-Pakistani dispute was fairly well in line with Soviet policy. At least in recent years, the Soviet Union has not desired a war between these neighboring powers, promising as it might be for the establishment of communist rule in one or the other. Although it profits from a state of tension, the Soviet Union is probably undesirous also of a real conflagration in the Near East, and has supported U.N. efforts to keep the conflict within bounds. However, the Soviet Union clearly prefers that the peacemaker should be itself, as in Kosygin's Tashkent mediation between India and Pakistan in 1965; and apparently it would prefer a Near East settlement (so far as it desires any settlement) to be negotiated outside the U.N.

A related area is disarmament, which the U.N. has always sponsored. As a focus and channel of disarmament negotiations, the U.N. has encouraged hopes of moderating or checking the Union has been disposed to make sweeping and outwardly attrac-arms race, an apparent Soviet goal. Since the 1920's, the Soviet tive disarmament proposals. The purpose has been in part propa-gandistic, or, as the communists have stated it, to show up the inability of the "capitalist" states to disarm, and in part political, to divide potentially anti-Soviet forces. The Soviet Government, because of its closed nature and the importance to it of secrecy, has been reluctant to accept controls or verification except, presum-ably, after the disarmament measures have been carried out. For this reason, and because both sides have been more fearful of loss of position than desirous of disarmament, the interminable discus-sions since 1946 have led to no basic change in the situation. The Russians have a real interest in some limitation of armaments however. Soviet leaders apparently recognize that the world be-comes more dangerous as arms are piled up indefinitely, and eco-nomic planners may be clamoring for the resources diverted to war industry. Especially in the time of Khrushchev's optimism regarding Soviet capacities for outperforming its rivals econom-ically, it seemed desirable to bring about at least an atmosphere of disarmament, in which nonmilitary means of expansion might have fuller play. Although Khrushchev also tried to use military threats for political advantage, rattling rockets over Berlin and other issues, the West has probably failed to explore adequately Soviet offers of disarmament in 1955 and after.

Soviet writers credit the United Nations with pushing the "imperialist" powers toward acceptance of broad principles of disarmament.[26] For serious negotiation, however, the Russians have lately seemed strongly to prefer dealing directly with the United States. Thus, in December 1968, the Soviet Union joined the United States to oppose reactivization of the General Assembly's dormant Disarmament Commission as proposed by a number of smaller states. and recent talks between Washington and Moscow on strategic arms limitation have been entirely outside the U.N.

It remains doubtful, in any case, whether the Soviet Union could afford any substantial degree of disarmament. Within the theoretical framework of Soviet political thinking, viewing history as class conflict, it would be very hazardous for the "socialist" society to disarm (even if there were no danger from Communist China) in a predominantly class-inimical world. Moreover, the military establishment seems to play a larger role in the Soviet Union than in the United States, as it receives a greater proportion of the national income and there are less effective constitutional means for the citizenry to make itself felt. The extensive glorification of the military and military-patriotic virtues in official Soviet media would indicate that the armed forces may be a very important, perhaps indispensable, part of the modern Soviet political system, the more vital as the persuasiveness of ideology declines.

A related utility to the Soviets of their presence in the United Nations is to hinder the utilization of this body against Soviet purposes. Ever since the civil war, when the Allied powers intervened and but for their lack of drive would doubtless have liquidated the Bolshevik government, the Soviet nightmare has been a concerted attack of "capitalist" powers. If the Soviet Union were to withdraw, the danger of the United Nations becoming an anti-Soviet coalition would be great; the lesson of Korea is not forgotten. Despite the humiliations it suffered, Stalinist Russia always saw the utility of working inside the organization; the contrast with the arrogant withdrawals of Germany, Japan, and Italy from the League of Nations in the 1930's is instructive. Even if there were no fear of the United Nations' becoming an anti-communist league, the Soviet Union has every reason to remain inside to hinder the U.N.'s development into a real international power, a development for which the Soviets have an antipathy.

Hardly separable from working in the U.N. to prevent its being turned against the Soviet Union is using it as a means of raising the world standing of the Soviet Union and its political system, which would presumably enhance the struggle for the final victory of socialism. The U.N. is an excellent place to present the Soviet view of the world to diplomats of nearly all the countries of the world, with many of which the Soviet Union still has no diplomatic relations. As a Soviet commentator put it, "The U.N. General Assembly is the world's highest political rostrum. . . . Everything said in the Assembly goes round the world and is commented upon everywhere, generating fresh currents of thought among men and working on their frame of mind." [27] From considerable indifference during the first decade of the United Nations' existence, the Soviet Union has come to considerable appreciation of its possibilities and to skill in using them. The importance of the U.N. for Soviet foreign policy rose especially from 1953 to 1960, when Khrushchev briefly made it the focus of his diplomacy with his invitation to all heads of state to meet with him there for a mass "summit." It has receded since then, as Soviet interests and ambitions in the Third World have changed, but the businesslike Brezhnev-Kosygin government is not inclined to neglect any means of forwarding its interests.

The Soviet Union has been prepared to support in the U.N. practically any issue that seemed to weaken the "capitalist" West and encourage the separation of the non-European world from Western influence. The utility of this stratagem to the communist cause and the Soviet Union has been exaggerated because of the Leninist theory of imperialism, according to which the stability of capitalism in the leading Western powers is attributable to their exploitation of the colonial and semicolonial lands. But there has been a ready-made set of antagonisms between the richer Western powers and the less developed countries on which Soviet diplomacy could play; and the U.N.—with its large majority of less developed countries—has been an obvious channel for this attack.

The largest part of the Soviet propaganda offensive in the U.N. has consequently been directed to the many poorer, mostly new states. To them, the simple emotional tune of anti-imperialism has been musical, and they have been prepared to listen when Soviet spokesmen blamed the outdated "capitalist" world order and the selfishness of the economically dominant nations for their poverty and impotence in an age of technological miracles. The Russians strongly encourage nationalism—meaning usually anti-Westernism—in states searching for a national identity; their advocacy of state ownership has struck a responsive chord in countries anxious to develop rapidly by state planning, distrustful of foreign capital, and sometimes seeking excuses for expropriation of Western-owned enterprises. To solve their problems, the Soviets maintained, they needed only to eliminate the "exploitation" by "monopoly capital" and follow the methods that raised Russia from a status like their own to economic and political power. This message had the additional attraction that it downgraded the economic assistance given by the Western powers and relieved the Soviet Union of the moral obligation to furnish aid itself through U.N. programs—the basic purpose of which was seen by the Soviets as the prevention of socialization. Largely or entirely leaving behind less palatable aspects of Soviet ideology, like atheism and class struggle, the Soviets have appealed to nations impatient with details and practical difficulties with lofty declarations, flattering to the weak and poor. By comparison, the ideological appeal of the United States has been dry and inappropriate to the emotions of the poorer two thirds of humanity.

Delegates of less developed countries have noted at times that the Soviet Union was more interested in making a propaganda case than in forwarding programs in which they were interested, and many of them have been aware of less attractive features of the Soviet economic and political system. Anti-Westernism began wearing somewhat thin after a decade or more. Socialism nowhere proved a panacea for economic ills, and in the cases of Ghana and Guinea it failed badly. However, Soviet intervention in U.N. debates must be counted fairly successful, not so much in praising things Soviet as in touching sore points and focusing upon the shortcomings of the Western powers; not so much in selling specific Soviet policies as in promoting a general Marxist interpretation of events. The Soviet posture in the U.N. has probably done much to make many nations more sympathetic to the Soviet Union and more receptive to its initiatives for bilateral cultural, economic, and political relations.

The Russians have at times had considerable hope for the United Nations as a means of swinging large parts of the world toward their side. Within their political philosophy, however, the Russians can at best regard the U.N. as a usable expedient. The Soviet Union, with the domain for which it has assumed political responsibility and in practice supreme control, itself represents an international system, of which ethnic Russians are only half of the population. This multinational system is legitimized by a universalist creed of class conflict and exclusive historical destiny. Marxism-Leninism, which has proved itself an integral part of the Soviet political order by its persistence through more than half a century, implies that such organizations as the United Nations are useless or worse than useless. If Soviet practice has usually been dictated more by practical than theoretical considerations, it remains true that the Soviet state has its own "proletarian" internationalism and universalist pretensions, for which the United Nations is competitive and inherently bad.

In World War I, Lenin contended that war could be ended only by the overthrow of the capitalism that he saw as the cause of imperialism, international anarchy, and conflict. Subsequently, the Soviets held that the League of Nations could do nothing to bring peace, which could be assured only by socialism and a new world order which would engulf the nations in the natural unity of the world proletariat. For practical reasons, the Soviet Union joined the League in 1934 and cooperated with and supported it, although with more verbal intensity than practical effect. But this relationship of convenience lasted hardly four years, while there seemed some prospects of the Soviet Union's entering collective security arrangements with Britain and France. Otherwise, the Soviet Union has invariably damned all schemes of world order— indeed, all moves toward regional integration also—not patronized by itself. "Cosmopolitanism" is a foul term in the Soviet lexicon. Any idea that a unifying approach could do any good, unless it is under the aegis of Soviet Marxism-Leninism, is anathema. It is unlikely that the Soviet Union will ever favor a unification even sponsored by communist parties unless it is the major partner, as Tito learned in 1948, when he made gestures toward a patently sensible Balkan union.

The United Nations is not only competitive with Soviet supranationalism, "proletarian internationalism," and the world communist movement; it is inherently antagonistic. For the Soviets, struggle (within limits) is basically good and to be fostered; "world law" (with practical qualifications) is a reactionary notion designed to hinder revolutionary transformation, and though the

device may be used to restrain other powers, it has no real application to Soviet conduct. Law, internal and external, is frankly held
an extension of politics. Relations among "socialist" states are
subject to different and more "progressive" rules, as was often asserted and emphasized in 1968. If the U.N. economic-develop-
mental program is successful, this is all to the bad; not only does
it rival Soviet bilateral programs, but it is oriented to a free and
open social order, means acceptance of a reformist and ameliorative approach, and excludes the need for violence and radical
transformation.

It seems to the Soviet political observer that, "socialism" being the only real cure for the world's ills, U.N. organs benefit only
the "imperialists" and "monopoly capitalists" as they work for the
stabilization of the present social order and foster a mentality of
harmonization, denying the class struggle. The basic Soviet-Lenin-
ist approach to the problems of the noncommunist world is not to
solve them but to use them. If the Western powers wish to promote "stable government, competent and honest administration,
favorable attitudes toward foreign investment, better spreading of
tax burden, growth of agricultural production," etc., this can only
be derided as neocolonialism.[28] The Soviets are driven to de-
nounce equally price instability and any schemes for its ameliora-
tion, both being regarded as the exploitation of monopoly capital.
It is understandable that Soviet voluntary contributions to U.N.
programs (about 3 per cent of the total, compared to a Soviet share
of the regular budget of 17.41 per cent) are only enough to give
entrée and some appearance of participation. The Soviet political
system is incompatible with any idea of non-Marxist-Leninist
world community.

The Soviet Union opposes any development of the United
Nations that might lead in the direction of world federalism. For
the Soviet Union the United Nations is nothing but a contractual
arrangement among sovereign powers. The U.S.S.R. has regularly
contested on grounds of national sovereignty any extension of
U.N. faculties, and it has been the only member to insist repeatedly on the right of withdrawal.[29] The U.N. is part of the bourgeois world, by hypothesis hostile and insincere. Neutralism may
be recognized for tactical reasons, but it has no place in Soviet

philosophy. Since objective and class factors must prevail, the goodwill of bourgeois states, even if real, can have only limited importance. The "capitalist" analysis of world events must necessarily be biased and lacking the true insight of Marxist-Leninists. The only real arguments are the facts of power, for which Soviet leaders have always shown respect. As a deliberative constitutional body, the U.N. is repugnant to the absolutist Soviet political mentality. Stalin and Khrushchev were fairly frank in their condescension for weak powers. As Khrushchev said, "Even if the vote were 99 to 1 against the Soviet Union, the Soviet Union will have no part of anything we do not approve." [30] There is no reason to suppose that the present leaders, if less outspoken, have a different view.

It is questionable whether the Soviet Union could hold together its various nationalities and sustain its dominion of Eastern Eruope without substantial military forces, and radical disarmament is hence unrealistic for the Soviet political system. Likewise, it may be necessary for the stability of the Soviet domain to cultivate a degree of tension with the outside. This is the practical essence of Marxism-Leninism as applied to the world scene: the "capitalist" states are viewed as intrinsically hostile to the "socialist" states, as is elaborated at enormous length and repetitiveness in all Soviet communications media, directly and by implication. The "bourgeois" ruling classes can only hate and seek to destroy the "workers' state," and any seemingly friendly moves they may make are to be attributed not to possible good intentions but to their weakness against the "socialist" states or their own masses. The United Nations, still basically representative of "capitalist" interests, aims at removal of tension and the development of understanding among nations; as applied to the "socialist" states this is an insidious form of aggression.

This means not only that the purposes of the United Nations cannot be the same as those of the Soviet Union except in limited areas, but also that real trust is undesirable, to be excluded. There is no large area of contact between the United Nations and the Soviet people. Arms control, requiring the penetration of Soviet society by an external and presumably hostile political body, is very dimly regarded. Other states have excluded what they regarded as United Nations intrusion on their territory, e.g., South Africa, and India in the Goa question. No "socialist" state has admitted any sort of U.N. inspection. Politically, the United Nations structure and functioning are a challenge to the essence of the Soviet system; extensive collaboration with its economic and social programs could only undermine Soviet economic and social doctrine.

The United Nations must influence the few Soviet citizens in direct contact with it, although they are fairly well insulated by their elite status and there is no question of Soviet citizens really becoming part of an international civil service. The Soviet people receive very little information about the United Nations, except as the struggle of good and evil goes on within it. U.N. efforts in favor of "freedom of information" are regarded as a cover for anticommunist propaganda.[31] Until 1955, the Soviet Union declined even to furnish statistics for U.N. dissemination, although Soviet statistics are normally rather favorable to the government. Subsequently, there has been opened a United Nations information center in Moscow, but it is small and inconspicuous and, unlike such centers in noncommunist countries, is manned only by nationals of the host country.

A recent incident involving this center showed something of the significance of the United Nations for the Soviet Union. In June 1969, fifty-four Soviet citizens tried to send the United Nations a petition that they be allowed human rights guaranteed by the Universal Declaration of Human Rights, signed by the Soviet Union. The U.N. information center refused to forward the petition, although required to do so by standing instructions; the Soviet director followed not his international duty but the policies of his Government. A smuggled copy eventually reached the U.N. Human Rights Commission, but the signers were subjected to various measures of harassment, from loss of jobs to psychiatric confinement.[32]

It is not to be supposed that the Soviet Union takes its official ideology with absolute and literal seriousness and strives only for the "revolutionary transformation" of the world (as the old-time goal of "world revolution" has come to be restated), for which "Peaceful Coexistence" is only a tactic designed to gain time and disarm the enemy. On the other hand, it is not to be supposed that the much-repeated doctrines and the militant "ideological strengthening" of the Soviet people have merely domestic, mostly formal significance, while the Soviet state is motivated in its international relations quite as are ordinary and less pretentious polities. Both aspects are real and strong, the strength of one or the other being at times more apparent, in accordance with the urgency of internal-political needs or external exigencies. In the stress of World War II, Marxist ideology was not necessary for unification and legitimation, and it largely disappeared from view. When liberalization in Czechoslovakia seemed threatening in 1968, there was a great intensification of stress on ideology and the supremacy of "class" considerations over all else, a reversion toward the Stalinist position that there was no middle ground in the sharpening world struggle.

This is the fundamental ambivalence of Soviet relations with the West. The Western "capitalist" powers, or at least the more powerful of them, must be held theoretically to be completely hostile, and the Soviet realm must be protected from their influence. At the same time it is recognized to be desirable, even indispensable, to deal with them in a businesslike, perforce friendly way for many purposes. It is essential to work within the established order while dogmatically opposing it and at least theoretically striving to subvert it.

This ambivalence fully applies to Soviet relations with the United Nations, which is part of the theoretically temporary but evidently lasting truce between hostile worlds. Really to accept the U.N. and its goals would be a sacrifice of Soviet fundamentals; to reject it would mean foregoing many opportunities and would be detrimental to security. If the Soviet leaders become more concerned for security, one can be certain that they will look more to the U.N., just as Stalinist Russia briefly became a fervent champion of the League of Nations when it seemed that this might serve to organize opposition to Nazism. The rift with China led the Soviet Union to drop its opposition to amendment of the United Nations Charter in 1963. The utility of the U.N. also rises with optimism about making converts around the world, as Khrushchev hoped. On the contrary, if Soviet leaders sense little menace from the world without and little to be gained from trying to spread their influence, whilst feeling less secure in their grip at home, they can be expected to turn their backs on the United Nations. Similarly, they have something to gain by participating in an economic and social program the success of which would be disastrous to their expectations. The ordinary compromise is limited cooperation to check threats to the peace without willingness to support a real peacekeeping force, and in the developmental programs a cooperation that is more appearance than reality.

This uncertainty has doubtless limited the effectiveness of the Soviet Union in the United Nations, where Soviet influence has at best been much less than would correspond to Soviet power. It may also be surmised that on balance the United Nations has been of more harm than benefit to the Soviet-sponsored world movement, although probably not to the national interest of the Soviet Union as ordinarily conceived. The communists have always had great faith in the power of the message, and the flow is almost entirely from the Soviet Government through the U.N. and to the peoples of the world rather than from foreign governments to the Soviet people.

Yet the U.N. has helped to improve relations among many nations, to decrease frictions and dampen hostile feelings, particularly between the West and the less developed countries, the promising recruits for the Soviet cause. It has probably reduced the propensity to turn to communism as the only available alternative. It has also been clearly contrary to the Soviet interest that the U.N. has turned away to a considerable extent from the strictly political and security functions that Stalin wished for it in 1945 and has instead become an important shelter and meeting ground for a variety of international economic and social programs. It has come increasingly to bespeak a permanent noncommunist international system, the success of which can only detract from that of Lenin's movement.

In view of this, the Soviets may wonder if they get full value for their share of the U.N. budget, approximately half that of the United States. They have, however, always seen it as better to be in than out. The prestige of the U.N. and its near universality of membership—in striking contrast to that of the League of Nations—make it mandatory for the Soviet Union to seek the best means of working within it. Withdrawal would make sense only if the Soviet Union were practically to withdraw from world affairs, a contingency that is almost inconceivable. But the U.N. is and seems likely to remain of very little importance for Soviet policy. Mostly by its own choice, the Soviet Union has largely remained on the periphery of policy making within the U.N. administrative apparatus, while Soviet delegates have regularly emphasized national sovereignty (except where propaganda advantages were seen in moving for intervention, as in the case of the Portuguese colonies) and sought to hold down the U.N. budget. The Soviet Union remains a nonparticipant in a number of U.N. agencies, not only those dealing with commerce and international finance but even those handling agriculture and civil aviation. Perhaps the best measure of the real worth of the U.N. in Soviet eyes is the attention or lack of attention to it in major statements. Long Soviet tracts on foreign affairs make no or only incidental mention of it. The official Party Program of 1961, a document the size of a short book, quite ignored it. The lengthy declaration of the Moscow conference of communist parties in June 1969 also omitted reference to the U.N., although its theme was the struggle against "imperialism"; and major policy statements by Brezhnev or Gromyko mention the U.N. quite incidentally, if at all.

THE UNITED NATIONS AND AMERICAN PURPOSES

Soviet purposes and policies in the United Nations are complicated, but they are essentially simpler than those of the United States. The authoritarian state is not really monolithic, but in comparison with the swirling political currents of the big democratic state it usually seems like a single tidal flow. Soviet purposes are contradictory, but they represent a fairly sharp duality arising from the basic needs of the state. American purposes are multiform and fuzzy, as different interests and tendencies assert themselves in the pluralistic society; America does not speak with a single public voice.

The most obvious division in the American attitude toward the United Nations is the difference between the urges of the administration, which expounds and applies policy, and the Congress, which is called upon to finance and at times to check or sanction it. The executive branch has regularly taken the more internationalist view, seeing American interests as best served by the world order to which the U.N. should contribute. The Congress, partly in reflection of more conservative sectors of public opinion, has been more distrustful of the alien international organization and has wished to see clearly the immediate national interests served. The one has been more desirous of building up the U.N., the other to have it serve American foreign policy and particularly the anticommunist cause. Thus Congress attacked the Secretariat in 1952 for the employment of allegedly disloyal or communist-inclined American citizens, while the executive sought to smooth the issue. The Congress has been most insistent on American opposition to membership for Communist China over a period of many years, tying the hands of the administration and to some extent distorting the American position in the U.N. The Senate has been loath to ratify several innocuous humanitarian conventions for a decade or more, feeling that they might imply the world body had something to say about American domestic concerns. These include conventions on genocide and forced labor, which might be expected to be much more embarrassing to the Soviet Union which has not hesitated to subscribe to them. There was feeling in Congress that the bond issue for Congo operations meant that the United States was paying more than its share, while the State Department was better aware how well the peacekeeping mission served American policy. In 1961, Congressional anger seriously embarrassed the American delegation by demanding that it oppose a small technical assistance project for Cuba, thereby endeavoring, contrary to basic American principles, to introduce political considerations into the economic program. The Congress resented any American money going to help Castro, but the executive perceived that it would have been quite disadvantageous in the long run to raise a storm and perhaps endanger the whole program as well as tarnish the American image with the less developed countries over a minor matter. In countless cases it must be assumed that the administration would have proposed different or larger programs but for the conviction that Congress would not lend the necessary backing.

Some sectors of public opinion have, of course, been much more hostile to the U.N., holding it to be more or less communist-dominated and anti-American. Xenophobic extremist groups have spread many paranoiac rumors of U.N. subversion or preparations for an attack on the United States. On the other hand, an important part of the American public, especially in intellectual circles, has been enthusiastic for the U.N., tending to consider it more as an ideal than as a human institution. Especially in the immediate aftermath of the World War, excessive hopes were held for it, in the American fashion of expecting utopia as the reward of the great struggle. Since then, it has probably been true that American public opinion has paid more attention, mostly favorable, to the United Nations than that of any other great power.[33] The support of the American public for that organization has, however, been considerably eroded in the past decade by the divergence of interests between this country and the U.N. majority and the failure of the latter to stand by the United States in what it considered matters of principle.

The dichotomous American feelings toward the U.N. have been remotely parallel to those of the Soviet Union: on the one hand, lofty, slightly xenophobic attitudes in the imperial spirit, with distrust for the universal body so far as it seems uncontrollable and alien; on the other, desire to seek fulfillment of American purposes in cooperation with the world community. Like the Soviet Union, this country is allergic to any suggestion of infringement on its sovereignty; and the United States has some sense, usually very diffuse, of its special world mission. Both superpowers have suffered in the community of nations from a certain selfrighteousness, although this has ordinarily been more flagrant and offensive on the Russian side;

and the contention that American policy has been imperialistic has been a major asset of Soviet diplomacy in the United Nations. The United States has a sphere of influence in Latin America that might conceivably be compared with the Soviet one in Eastern Europe, although the differences are at least as marked as the resemblances. To some extent the Americans have followed the Russians in seeking to use the United Nations to sell the American "way of life." But the American ideology, if it can be called this, is less charming for the poor who dominate the U.N. numerically. The promotion of free enterprise and economic freedom, with lectures on the advantages of open systems and international exchanges, has signified to the poorer nations that their condition resulted simply from their failure to produce and that they had to welcome foreign capital and work harder to hope to improve themselves.

It is also to be remarked that the United States has often failed to back up its moral commitment to the United Nations wih consistent support. American acceptance of the U.N. has depended to a large extent on the feeling that it was favorable to American interests and ideals, as it assuredly was for the first decade; it is not certain that the United States would be as patient as the Soviet Union in an unfriendly organization. It was at one time mooted that the United States might consider withdrawing if Communist China were let in. American financial support has been far more generous than Soviet, especially in voluntary contributions, but the return to this country has been at least proportionately great. It says a good deal about national priorities that expenditures for the U.N. are less than one quarter of 1 per cent of those of the Department of Defense; and that the United States has set itself, like the Soviet Union, rather firmly against increases of the U.N. budget. The United States, like the Soviet Union but with less reason, has consistently preferred bilateral to international economic aid, and it freely disregarded the International Atomic Energy Agency which was launched by President Eisenhower with great fanfare. The United States has also undercut the prestige and usefulness of the U.N. by by-passing it diplomatically. In the Korean War and in the Congo crisis United States and U.N. policy fairly well coincided, but in the former the United States unwisely went its own way when purposes diverged. For the most part, the United States has met crises alone or in consultation with allies with no or only marginal reference to the U.N., as in Berlin, Guatemala, Lebanon, Cuba, and Vietnam. Particularly in the last case, there has been an inclination to bring in the U.N. only as a measure of desperation when diplomacy and military action failed. Likewise when in the latter 1950's and the years after 1960 the United States was improving relations with the Soviet Union, the U.N. was given very little share in the generation of the atmosphere of détente. It has been said that while the Soviet Union acquired an empire from the war, the United States gained an international organization. If so the Russians have made more purposeful use of their acquisition than have the Americans.

The suitability of the U.N. for American purposes in the world would seem great. Its help in the cold war might be counted as equivalent to a number of divisions in checking communist expansionism in Iran, Greece, Korea, and the Congo, mostly by certifying facts as seen by the most trusted political body in the world, and giving legitimacy to the Western position. This utility has greatly diminished; if the U.N. could do little about Hungary in 1956 it could do practically nothing about Czechoslovakia in 1968. It seems unlikely that the U.N. will take a strong stand on future East–West issues except possibly in case of the most flagrant aggression, especially against a country of the Third World. The U.N. may still, however, have some effect in moderating Soviet conduct. The fact that there exists a world tribunal where nearly all nations are present is important even if it can do nothing but talk; it at least makes for greater awareness of world public opinion and so for a little more sense of responsibility. It is especially helpful that the presence of the U.N. makes it a little more difficult for the Soviet Union to move into local quarrels.

The U.N. may also be called upon to discomfit the Soviet political system in its less enlightened aspects. The U.N. forum has been less useful to the West than to the Soviet side as a means of propaganda; the message of the less authoritarian powers is not so clear-cut, they are not as well oriented to making use of propaganda, and they have many other private and official channels to nearly all states. But just as the Soviet delegates have devoted much time to denouncing the ills of capitalism, from unemployment to pornography, the United States can only gain from supporting U.N. positions regarding genocide, forced labor, and civil and political rights, which all delegations must profess to support, and might well call for more investigation into their fulfillment. No body can pass resolutions as well as the U.N. about the rights of all states to manage their own affairs and enjoy their own political and economic system without interference, and about the inadmissibility of military intervention. The ability of the United States to call for fulfillment of these resolutions has been curtailed, as seen by many U.N. members, by its intervention in Vietnam. Yet the general principles of nonintervention should be entirely advantageous to this country. It is quite possible, moreover, that the anticolonial issue may turn strongly against the Soviet Union. With the exception of the Portuguese, the European colonial empires are a receding memory. Only the Russian empire remains, supplemented by the domination of most of Eastern Europe. In a world otherwise free, the U.N., based on principles of self-determination and representative of more than a hundred states jealous of their independence, might exert some pressure toward its transformation.

More broadly, the U.N. has served the American interest in lessening tensions and moderating conflicts, to some extent between the superpowers, to a greater degree between smaller countries. It cannot solve basic issues, like the fundamental antagonism of the American and Soviet political systems or the irreconcilable clash of Arab and Israeli demands. The value of the U.N. as a diplomatic meeting ground has already been mentioned; if the public and televised debates lead to no changes of position, the U.N. locale is nevertheless suitable for private bargaining. The U.N. may serve as a vehicle of compromise in another way, as in the Cuban crisis: not only was U Thant the only mediator available, but when the superpowers had essentially resolved the dispute it was easier to come to agreement on the basis of a United Nations role; it was a face-saver on both sides to propose United Nations control, even if this was not in fact implemented.

Disarmament is a subject to which the U.N. has paid much attention practically since its inception; if it has made little progress, it still remains a useful adjunct so far as the great powers are willing to negotiate toward reducing the arms burdens. It furnishes locale and auspices for discussions, and such agencies as the International Atomic Energy Agency (IAEA) can be formed within its framework. It is important for prospects of a general acceptance of the treaty to halt the spread of nuclear weapons that it was approved by the General Assembly. Moreover, the smaller powers can apply some pressure through the U.N. for disarmament of the very great. This is not only because of their fear of war. Being militarily impotent, they prefer a less armed world; and they have hopes that if less were spent on arms more would be spent on aid to them.

As the noncommunist world is free and diverse, it is certain to face quarrels; there is no better agency than the U.N., imperfect as it is, to exert pressure for moderation and hinder their escalating into Soviet–American conflicts. Its presence helps at least a little to keep the superpowers at a distance, as in Suez, Cyprus, and the Congo. It is a suitable factfinder and mediator, by far the most broadly acceptable umpire because of its prestige and universality and the openness and international democracy of its debates. Only the U.N. can man cease-fire lines and (albeit perhaps futilely, as in the Near East conflict) report violations. It serves to some extent as a nonmilitary outlet for anger, as nations can vent some of their passions in its halls. The United Nations is blamed for its failures, even for its incomplete successes, but receives little credit for the troubles it averts. One can only guess that the world would be much more dangerous if it did not exist.

The U.N. also contributes, although usually feebly and perhaps imperceptibly, toward making the kind of world that the United States as a country and the large majority of Americans desire. The U.N. stands for a world of independence and diversity, in harmony with broad American ideals. A symbol of the equality and sovereignty of nations, it stands for the legitimacy of nations and their right to exist. It is opposed to violence and disorder, yet it can facilitate peaceful change, as in decolonization, toward a more satisfactory and presumably more stable order. It is a living advertisement, so far as it is respected, of the democratic society, with its majority rule, equality of the weak, free debate and confrontation of ideas and interests, and constitutional order. It is wholly contrary to the Soviet demand for conformity in "class" struggle.

The idea of the U.N.'s maturing into a powerful agent of collective security was undercut by its failure to enforce the financial responsibility of members. But so far as America has any hopes of building toward world community, they rest largely on the United Nations, the need for whose specialized activities grows with the progress of technology and the interrelatedness of nations. The U.N. has or can create a great variety of facilities for coping with international problems of all sorts. The need can only continue to grow, and habits of international cooperation could be strengthened indefinitely as the U.N. became more and more important for practical purposes. The U.N. might also do much toward developing sounder economic relations and to reducing the gap between rich and poor nations. Although the United States, like the Soviet Union but to a much less degree, has been averse to turning over any large part of its foreign aid program to a body that it cannot control, the United Nations is a desirable channel for aid, especially to countries fearful or sensitive about bilateral programs with the West. It is also suitable as a conduit for capital investment, avoiding the national label and the suspicion of capitalist exploitation, reducing psychological barriers and the sense of inferiority of recipient nations. The American delegate to the United Nations not long ago stated that multilateral aid better served the United States than bilateral, chiefly because it was less political and caused less resentment.[34] No other agency is so well prepared to undertake the control and management of the threatened but increasingly important resources of the oceans. If humanity is to cope with worldwide pollution and conservation needs, responsibility must surely rest with the United Nations. The U.N. may also help to meet the burden of uncontrolled population growth. American approaches to birth control are often stigmatized as imperialistic; the patently disinterested body expressive of the interests of mankind should be able best to make its assistance generally welcome.

The outlook for such growth is at best cloudy. If the development of the economic and social aspects of the U.N. is eminently in the American interest, it is less in that of the Soviets, who have ample ideological reason to abhor an evolution toward a noncommunist world community. The antithesis of communist and Western, or of Soviet and American, political purposes sharply limits the potential of the United Nations, which can undertake little without the assent of the two political leaders. In the current militancy of the Soviet ideological posture and the pervasive emphasis on struggle, it seems doubtful that the present Soviet leadership will go so far toward broad cooperation with the United States as did Khrushchev, who found Eisenhower to be a "man of peace." It is symptomatic that the Soviet Union denounced, in September 1969, the proposal that the U.N. act against aerial hijackings. The American mood in a very different way has turned from the United Nations. The sense of frustration abroad and the urge to pull back and concentrate on domestic troubles, generated largely but not entirely by the Vietnam war, is reflected in increased indifference to the United Nations and the needs of the countries that dominate it numerically. With reason, the President of the Assembly, Angie Brooks, opened the 1969 session with an unaccustomed lament: "Whoever is at fault, the sad fact is that with governments sometimes pursuing one policy for national use and seemingly another for use in the United Nations, we have not achieved the strength with which the Charter in its totality endowed us."

It is possible, however, that the world and the United States may come to a better appreciation of the possibilities of the United Nations. No nation can divorce itself from the problems and dangers of this world. If America wishes to reduce involvement and responsibility, it could do no better than to advance through the United Nations basic policies that are in the interests of the large majority of states. If the U.N. is dominated by sometimes unrealistic majorities of weak powers, this may at times be irritating, as when in March 1970 the United States felt obliged to resort to its first veto against a resolution calling for the use of force in the Rhodesian case. But the United Nations is the nearest to the conscience of mankind, and the small powers for the most part urge the big ones to do what the latter probably ought to do for other reasons but are politically inhibited from doing, especially to disarm and to move more effectively to narrow the immense gap between rich and poor nations. Most of all, of course, they seek to secure their own independence, which is entirely in the American interest.

The United Nations seems unable to solve important political problems, but these may be gradually submerged if nations are led to cooperate in the practical tasks of assuring a livable world. If civilization goes forward, making states ever more interdependent, a universal organization must become more and more vital, an indispensable part of any progressive world order. The United Nations' potentialities are largely unrealized and in practice feeble; but the weak creature is the best in being. In its present shape, the institution is not entirely to the taste of the United States, but neither is the contemporary world to which this country must adapt. An international organization is necessary; it was possible to bring one into being in the aftermath of World War II, but it would probably not be possible to agree on a new one today. Whatever the defects of the United Nations, there is no apparent alternative.

NOTES

1. James Byrnes, *Speaking Frankly* (New York, 1947), pp. 24, 37.
2. John G. Stoessinger, *The United Nations and the Superpowers* (New York, 1965), passim.
3. Byrnes, *op. cit.,* pp. 78, 301.
4. Harold K. Jacobson, *The U.S.S.R. and the U.N.'s Economic and Social Activities* (Notre Dame, Ind., 1963), p. 240.
5. Alvin Z. Rubinstein, *The Soviets in International Organizations* (Princeton, 1964), p. 13.
6. Alexander Dallin, *The Soviet Union at the United Nations* (New York, 1962), p. 29.

7. Rubinstein, *op. cit.*, p. 352.
8. G. I. Morozov et al., eds. *Spetsializirovannyie uchrezhdeniia OON v sovremennom mire* (Moscow, 1967), p. 46.
9. Rubinstein, *op. cit.* p. 41.
10. A. Nekrasov, "The Soviet Union Upholds the Economic Independence of the Emergent Nations," *International Affairs* (Moscow), May 1964, p. 51.
11. G. I. Morozov et al., *op cit.*, p. 37.
12. Lincoln P. Bloomfield, *The United Nations and U.S. Foreign Policy* (Boston, 1967), p. 52.
13. Trygve Lie, *In the Cause of Peace* (New York, 1954), p. 84.
14. Bloomfield, *op. cit.*, p. 70.
15. Alexander Dallin, *op. cit.*, p. 101.
16. Trygve Lie, *op. cit.*, p. 230.
17. Rubinstein, *op. cit.*, p. 274.
18. I. A. Kirilin, ed., *Istoriia mezhdunarodnykh otnoshenii*, Vol. III 1945–1967 (Moscow, 1967), pp. 477–478.
19. *United Nations Chronicle*, IV, 5 (May 1967), 11.
20. *United States in World Affairs*, 1964, p. 315.
21. *New York Times*, January 29, 1969.
22. United States interest in the undeveloped countries which dominate the U.N. numerically has waned markedly.
23. *Department of State Bulletin*, LX, 1563 (June 9, 1969), 494–496.
24. *Vneshniaia Torgovlia*, July 1969.
25. Kirilin, *op. cit.*, p. 477.
26. M. Lvov, "U.N.: Rostrum, Forum, Arena," *International Affairs* (Moscow), November 1963, pp. 10–16.
27. *Ibid.*, p. 11.
28. Morozov et al., *op. cit.*, p. 48.
29. Alexander Dallin, *op. cit.*, p. 31.
30. James J. Wadsworth, *The Glass House* (New York, 1966), p. 107.
31. Morozov et. al., *op. cit.*, p. 45.
32. *New York Times*, June 19, 1969.
33. Bloomfield, *op. cit.*, p. 3.
34. Charles W. Yost, *Department of State Bulletin*, XL, 1555 (April 14, 1969), p. 326.

THE SUPERPOWERS, THE U.N., AND DISARMAMENT: A VIEW FROM THE THIRD WORLD

Arthur Lall

The focus of attention here is a selective examination of the behavior of the two superpowers, the U.S.A. and the U.S.S.R., at the United Nations and its extended forms—particularly those relating to disarmament. It will point to certain conclusions as to the effectiveness of the influence of the United Nations on these two states—both juridically and through the urging of member states and the resolutions of U.N. organs. These conclusions must be tentative because the U.N. system is still incomplete. It does not yet embrace China nor Germany. Moreover, the full diplomatic capacities of the non-aligned states are still in an incipient stage. It will not be until the major nonaligned states have reached the point of takeoff, to use W. Rostow's phrase, that their influence will have matured. In reality they are still too dependent on the superpowers, mainly for their economic sustenance and in a measure for their security, to be fully nonaligned.

After almost a quarter of a century of seemingly unbridgeable opposition between the United States and the U.S.S.R., it now looks as if some of the undercurrents of policy and behavior, particularly in the quiet diplomacy that goes on in and around the U.N., are returning to the pristine assumptions of the beginning of that organization—primarily the assumption that the main allies of World War II would work together to keep a decent state of peace and order in our world.

Though events seem, in some respects, to be circling back to the desired beginning, the view just expressed has a somewhat brighter hue than the facts justify. This is so not because of any lack of facts, but rather because in the very first stages the assumption of a dominant role for the directing powers was implicit rather than explicit. The norms of conduct of states in an improved world order were accorded a primacy over the directing functions of a small group of states.

On the western side the basic assumptions were contained, in early and faint outline, in the Atlantic Charter of August 14, 1941. Looking forward to the end of the war, that Charter envisioned a system just for all nations, great and small, victor and vanquished; freedom of trade; freedom to choose the government that the people wanted; sovereign rights and self-government; freedom from fear and want for all peoples; a system of general security, the abandonment of the use of force by nations, and the lightening of the crushing burden of arms.[1] In brief, the Atlantic Charter was a document setting out norms of conduct for the future, norms that became the assumptions on which the U.N. was later built and its Charter written. These norms are still unexceptionable except for what Churchill wrote in on free access on equal terms to the raw materials of the world which smacks of the concept of exploitative "rights" of some nations as against others.

What is almost as important as the content of the norms and presumptive assumptions of the U.N. is who wrote the Atlantic Charter: the then two great Western powers. Not sufficient note has been taken of this fact in its relationship to the full meaning of the document that emerged. The Atlantic Charter was written without consultation with the leaders of the other states that were contributing to the defeat of Germany and Japan. (True, the United States was not yet formally in the Western alliance against the Axis, but it was drifting very near such association.) Here then was the assumption of the dominant role of the Great Powers which later found concrete expression in Chapter V of the U. N. Charter, particularly in

Articles 23 and 27. These articles translated what had been only implicit and perhaps secondary into something potentially not unlike the Holy Alliance after the defeat of Napoleon. This is not at all to say that the U.N. Charter is a replica of the 1815 arrangements, a precise case of international atavism. Not so. But it is necessary to point out that the concept of a directorate had apparently not changed very much. What had changed, in a measure, was the general context of international norms: freedom, human rights, self-determination, economic and social well-being, and so on which were also written into the Charter. However, in the last analysis the power to compel the international situation to go in one way rather than in another was envisaged as being vested in the wills of the chosen five who could presumably override the norms if they saw fit so to do.

We have now stated the basic dichotomy in the assumptions that underlie political conduct among states within the U.N. context: the norms of behavior prescribed for all member nations on the one hand, and the implicit right to disregard those norms on the other hand, with which five chosen powers have been endowed, a right that only two of the five have so far been able to sustain by the possession of an adequate power base or capacity, so that, in fact, only the United States and the U.S.S.R. can afford to mitigate, alter, or transgress the norms of conduct in order to safeguard their own interests. There are occasions and situations in which these two states might permit other states or groups of other states with which either of them is intimately associated also to flout a basic Charter norm of conduct.

A major primary assumption of both the United States and the U.S.S.R. from the very beginning of the U.N. era has been the necessity of attaining and then maintaining, by the possession of the requisite power, the capacity to reserve to themselves the operative right to act unilaterally in the protection and furtherance (though in this latter category of efforts grave risks could be involved) of their respective interests.

The past years of U.N. history have provided a fair number of territorial examples of the assertion of this right and capacity: Guatemala, Hungary, the Dominican Republic, and Czechoslovakia are so far some of the most striking cases in point.

There are other ways in which the right is asserted. One is by policies of military assistance to friends and allies, which subtly puts Charter norms in grave jeopardy. Another is by producing fantastic and still increasing levels of military preparedness, notwithstanding the reference in the Atlantic Charter to relief from the crushing burden of armament, and in the U.N. Charter to "the least diversion for armaments of the world's human and economic resources." [2]

The danger of trying to act for the furtherance of national interests becomes clear when either of the superpowers intrudes into the sphere of interest of the other. Cuba in 1961 was a case in point. It was bad enough—from the point of view of the United States—to have Castro reveal himself to be a communist, for this conflicted with President Kennedy's dictum that "Communist domination in this hemisphere can never be negotiated," [3] but it was intolerable that the military might of the Soviet Union should intrude into the geographical sphere of influence of the United States in the form of Soviet missiles located on Cuban territory. This Cuban-Soviet move led to the firm action of Kennedy to effect the extrusion of direct Soviet strength from Cuba—action that was fraught with the risks inherent in a situation created by the attempt of one superpower to extend its sphere of direct influence and control to the preserve of the other superpower.

The unforeseen military resistance to what began as a supposedly simple U.S. "cleanup" operation in South Vietnam arises precisely out of the fact that the other side regards this military venture by the United States as an intrusion into its sphere of influence. We may ignore for our purposes the complicating factor that on one side there are interests other than those of the Soviet Union—those of China and of Vietnam itself—involved. (Indeed, in almost every international situation there is a large number of national interests involved, but it is permissible to focus on the interests of some of the states concerned.) That the U.S.S.R. and its friends regard the United States' activities in Vietnam as an intrusion into their sphere of control is made explicit in the document entitled, "Tasks at the Present Stage of the Struggle Against Imperialism and United Action of the Communist and Workers' Parties and all Anti-Imperialist Forces" adopted by the international meeting of communist and workers' parties held at Moscow in June 1969: "The armed intervention in Vietnam holds a special place in the military and political designs of U.S. imperialism. The aggressor planned to destroy an outpost of socialism in Asia, block the way for the peoples of Southeast Asia to freedom and progress, strike a blow at the national liberation movement, and test the strength of the proletarian solidarity of the socialist countries and the working people of the whole world." [4]

In brief, the above citation means, "This is our sphere of interest, keep out." The risk of a wide war is heightened by the fact that the United States and many other countries do not agree that South Vietnam is within the Soviet (and allied) sphere of influence.

As to those cases in which the dominant events were clearly on territory within the sphere of influence of one side or the other—Guatemala, Hungary, the Dominican Republic, and Czechoslovakia—it is a striking fact that the efforts at U.N. involvement were either never very serious from the start or were allowed to peter out. True, in the case of Hungary the United States—and the Western powers in general—in the early stages mounted a full-blooded operation within the U.N. organs. But it is not irrelevant to ask to what extent that action would have been toned down had the Hungarian events not come on the heels of the Franco-British maneuver against Egypt in the Suez Canal area which ended disastrously for the western European powers. It was regarded as psychologically and politically necessary to make as much capital as possible out of the Hungarian occurrence in order to counterbalance the Suez mess. Certainly the strong statements of the Soviet representatives at the U.N. at the time of the Guatemalan and the Dominican situations were mainly for the record. There was no real attempt to pursue these matters and to make them issues of serious confrontation. Why? Because they were clearly within the geographic sphere of control of the United States.

In the case of Czechoslovakia there were strong U.S. speeches in the Security Council of the U.N., but no attempt was made even to place the issue on the agenda of the U.N. General Assembly. Again, clearly the reason was that the events had taken place in a country that had come to be regarded as falling within the sphere of control of the Soviet Union. More significant still is the fact, within the knowledge of some of the nonpermanent members of the Security Council at the time, that the United States showed no great determination, when the events broke in Prague, to call a meeting immediately of the Security Council. An attempt was made to get some of the nonpermanent members to bring it before the Council. Though this was done partly in order to show the U.S.S.R. that there was a wide range of opinion behind the projected castigation of its actions, the impression was that it would have been very acceptable if some one would come along and bell the cat.

In the general field of "interests" and "spheres of control" the case of the Middle East is a more complex one. Traditionally this has been an area of Western dominance rather than influence: the two concepts have to be clearly distinguished. Influence, in some not too obtrusive form, might be acceptable; dominance never is. Once Western European dominance in the Middle East was thrown off, the field was perhaps open for the ingress of other influences. To some extent—particularly economically (but economics is never entirely without political overtones)—this was even admitted to be the case by some of the states of the Middle East. However, John Foster Dulles was inept in regard to the Aswan dam and precipitated a chain of events that gave the Soviet Union, then under the guidance of the fast-thinking and ebullient Khrushchev, an opportunity to work for acceptable ingress for itself. In 1958 Dulles again slipped diplomatically in sending the marines to Lebanon in that once more the Soviets were able to take up a posture of being defenders of the rights of the Arabs—particularly the "progressive" Arabs.

By the time it came to the war of June 1967, the U.S.S.R. had definitely gained a foothold in the Middle East, though the United States too had influence with some of the Arab states as well as with the state of Israel. While the basic struggle in 1967 (as well as before and after) was between Israel and the

Arabs, it was also a struggle for the accommodation of what had come to be the "real interests"—as perceived by themselves —of both the United States and the Soviet Union. That struggle goes on and has become increasingly explicit. The U.N. forum for the settlement of the issue has been largely displaced, at any rate for the present crucial phase, by bilateral United States-Soviet talks and exchanges of documents on which a settlement might be based.

This implies a working assumption of the directional functions of the two great powers, which ties in with another implicit assumption in regard to the U.N. system so far as the United States and the Soviet Union are concerned. This is the dispensability of the U.N. organs in relation to these two powers. Of course, it was never the intention that the U.N. should take over all work connected with political and other settlements among states. Indeed, Article 33 of the U.N. Charter makes it explicit that member states should use every conceivable peaceful process—all kinds of negotiation, arbitration, judicial settlement, resort to regional agencies, "or other peaceful means of their own choice," before coming to the U.N. The last blanket phrase in Article 33.1 was intended to ensure that its scope would be exhaustive. It follows that there can be no quarrel with the tendency of the United States and the Soviet Union to attempt to deal with their own problems outside the U.N., always provided they use only peaceful methods and not force. Again, there is nothing against the superpowers', while keeping issues formally within the U.N., arriving at bilateral understandings, agreements, or treaties which they then pass through U.N. channels. It need scarcely be added that this procedure is appropriate only when the issues involved are genuinely bilateral and do not concern a larger number of states.

Within the U.N. membership it at first caused more surprise that the U.S.S.R. should now be willing—and often eager —to seek bilateral arrangements than that the United States should be willing to do so. This was so because in the past the U.S.S.R. had frequently, and over a considerable period of time, given the impression that it preferred a forum in which it could have the support of some of the other U.N. members. Indeed,

particularly in the period prior to the nuclear missile era, i.e.,
until about 1962–1963, one of the tenets of U.S.S.R. policy
had been the desirability of trying to even the diplomatic scales
by winning the support of the growing nonaligned membership of the U.N. It was in consonance with this policy that from
1954 onward, when India asked for a ban on the testing of
nuclear weapons at the U.N. General Assembly (an action initiated by Prime Minister Nehru), the Soviet Union would look
with sympathy on the test ban effort and would often vote for
the proposals of the nonaligned to set up machinery and arrangements to implement such a ban, whereas the United States
would demur. Similarly, on colonial issues the U.S.S.R. was
ready to back most of the proposals of the African and Asian
States. This phenomenon became so pronounced that some studies
came to the plausible but essentially mistaken conclusion that
the Indian delegation, for example, more often voted for the
U.S.S.R. than for the U.S.A. In fact what was happening was
that it was the U.S.S.R. which was voting for the Indian delegation's proposals and those of the other nonaligned states. If
one took as a starting point the proposals emanating from the
United States and its allies on the one hand, and those emanating
from the Soviet Union and its allies on the other hand, the facts
were that the nonaligned tended to abstain on most of the proposals of the communist states while many of them voted for at
least some of the Western proposals. They did this in spite of
the consistent support that they got from the communist states
on issues that they (the nonaligned) regarded as important.

At times the Soviet Union has insisted on advocating more
radical measures than the Asian or even the African states. For
example, in the middle fifties when most of the nonadministering
states on the U.N. Trusteeship Council were pressing the administering states to join with them in formulating timetables
for the completion of the process of advancement to statehood of
colonial territories, the Soviet delegate in the Council invariably
took the more radical position that there was no question of a
timetable because colonialism was inherently bad and had to be
liquidated immediately. In 1960, it was Mr. Khrushchev who
surprised the U.N. world including the nonaligned and others

by proposing a declaration on immediate independence for all colonial countries and peoples. The declaration was adopted by the U.N. General Assembly by an overwhelming majority vote [Resolution 1514 (XV)].

More recently (1967 and thereafter), the U.S.S.R. has generally maintained a more radical position than the African states on the question of South-West Africa (Namibia). Thus at the Fifth Special Session of the General Assembly as many as 79 anti-colonial states mainly from Africa, Asia and Latin America, urged acceptance of the creation of a U.N. Council to administer the territory but the U.S.S.R. advocated an immediate grant of independence and refused to vote for the 79-state resolution. Incidentally the United States too, along with the other Western states, abstained in the vote. For them the proposal went too far, rather than not far enough. The resolution was adopted [2248 (S-V)] but has remained inoperative. Since then the U.S.S.R. has maintained its position on immediate independence for the South-West Africa territory.

To return however to the issue of bilateralism on the part of the superpowers, what explained even as far back as the late fifties, and explains now, the keenness of the Soviet Union for direct agreements with the United States is that like all states it tends to the view that the most satisfactory negotiations are those between the parties directly concerned. The agreements or understandings arrived at as a result of such negotiations have a better chance of continuing in force than those reached as a result of third party efforts of judicial settlement. The degree of validity of this rule tends to be in direct proportion to the power of the parties involved and to the closeness of their power levels. In other words, today it is most valid in respect to the United States and the U.S.S.R.

There have been many cases of the exercise of the right of the superpowers to lift negotiations out of multilateral U.N. forums into the secrecy of their own bilateral efforts. This right has been exercised whether or not the subject matter concerned them alone or also other states.

The U.N., the Test Ban Conferences, the Eighteen-Nation Disarmament Committee, all discussed a test ban for some nine years, but when a partial agreement was reached it was, in fact, reached bilaterally (August 1963), though for good form the British were also represented. It caused resentment at the 18-Nation Disarmament conference that the efforts of the members there—particularly those of the eight nonaligned—were not significantly acknowledged in August 1963. It was once again bitterly resented by the rank and file of the membership of the U.N. Committee on the Peaceful Uses of Outer Space that they first learned from the newspapers that the United States and the U.S.S.R. had reached agreement (December 1966) on the terms of a treaty on the peaceful uses of outer space. It also caused deep resentment in the summer of 1969 that the United States and the U.S.S.R. should reach bilateral agreement, without any consultation with the other members of the Eighteen-Nation Disarmament Committee, on the expansion of that body by eight additional members. The nonaligned states protested in private, not against the principle of expansion or against the countries selected, but against the highhanded manner in which they were confronted with a decision taken by the two great powers as if the regulation, control, and lessening of arms were matters of interest to them alone. There had been no consultation with the other members of the Committee, no taking them into confidence. The "aggrieved" members of the Committee demanded an informal off-the-record session on July 30, 1969, at which they expressed themselves firmly and even trenchantly on the lack of common courtesy, and much else, involved in a procedure whereby they, as members of the committee, were not in any way included in the consultations regarding its expansion. But the superpowers were deaf to these complaints. Indeed, there will be no mention in the records of the Committee that this meeting was held.[5]

Earlier (1967–1968), the United States and the U.S.S.R. had similarly acted, without much prior consultation, to agree between themselves on the text of a draft treaty on the nonproliferation of nuclear weapons. This was regarded by many other states as more than merely surprising. It was regarded as dictatorial because the proposed treaty placed onuses and restrictions mainly on the nonnuclear powers. Not a few of the nonnuclear powers whose security and international standing would be affected by the proposed treaty could with validity claim a larger or at least equal say in world affairs and a larger or at least equal stake in peace in comparison with at least two of the present nuclear powers. True, the superpowers made minor modifications in their draft treaty, but these met only some of the peripheral demands of a few states. The main criticisms were left largely unheeded.

The two superpowers contend that the Eighteen-Nation Disarmament Committee (now known as the Conference of the Committee on Disarmament) is not a U.N. organ but merely a body which they—just the two of them—have created to consider, and, to the extent they desire, negotiate disarmament issues. A plausible technical case can be made in support of this view. But the technicalities apart, the substantive aspect of this view is of enormous relevance to an accurate assessment of the attitude of the superpowers toward the U.N., and to a full understanding of their basic assumptions in regard to conduct in the organization. The U.N. Charter states in Article 26 that the Security Council "shall be responsible for formulating, with the assistance of the Military Staff Committee . . . a system for the regulation of arms." This clause reflects the spirit of the words in the Atlantic Charter about "the establishment of a wider and permanent system of general security." It is the clear intention of the U.N. Charter that the organization should strive to realize disarmament. Moreover, though the superpowers are in a category of their own in respect of military might, disarmament, the regulation of arms, and the setting up of a system of international security are all sorely needed for the well-being of the other states with many times the number of people than the superpowers. More particularly it can be forcefully argued that the less wealthy states should be encouraged to take part in disarmament negotiations because they can ill afford an international system that encourages the squandering of their scant resources on expensive modern armament. Therefore, for factual considerations as well as because of the relevant Charter provisions, it is clearly appropriate that disarmament should be truly an international subject, within the U.N. framework, and that it should be negotiated primarily in and through U.N. bodies. Of course, from time to time regional bodies and bilateral discussions could also contribute to the U.N.'s efforts in regard to this core issue.

It is in keeping with the primacy of importance that the U.N. must and does attach to disarmament that the very first resolution adopted by the U.N. General Assembly was related to this topic.[6] Of such urgency was this matter deemed to be that the General Assembly acted on it even before turning to the immediate problems of structure, organization, rules and regulations. The whole of U.N. history reinforces the cardinal importance that member states attach to the effort to work out an acceptable system for the reduction of armaments in our world.

It is in the light of these factors that consideration should be given to the substance of the claim of the United States and the U.S.S.R. that the Eighteen-Nation Disarmament Committee is not a U.N. body. Clearly, whatever the technical arguments in favor of the view of the superpowers, that view is in substance not sustainable. If the other members of the U.N. took it seriously, and they do not, they would be obliged to create another disarmament negotiating body and invite the superpowers to join it. But this has not become necessary. Although, in order to preserve their freedom of action, the big two continue to maintain that the Disarmament Committee is not a U.N. body, they do, as cochairmen of the Committee,[7] report to the General Assembly; they make solemn statements to the General Assembly as to what they propose to do at the Committee; they join in the debates on their reports to the General Assembly; and they vote on and entertain the resolutions of the Assembly containing directives to the Disarmament Committee. It is, of course, quite another matter as to whether, and if so to what extent, these resolutions of the Assembly are heeded.

What emerges very strongly, then, in regard to the conduct of both the U.S.A. and the U.S.S.R., is the independence from the U.N. that both claim and, in considerable degree, practice. In each case this independence has a fairly clear geographical ambit, while in certain areas of the world the two states are willing to signal each other bilaterally. Apart from the geographical aspect of this independence—that is, independence within a territorial region—there is its vital-interest aspect—freedom of action on issues they deem important, i.e., disarmament and arms control. The assumption of both that they have a right to such independence of action as they require for their own purposes is undoubtedly the most significant of the assumptions that the United States and the U.S.S.R. make in regard to the United Nations.

A correlative assumption is that the U.N. is, for them, a forum and not a force. So far as they are concerned this is, of course, realistic. The U.N. is not in a position to coerce either of them, and certainly such of their actions as those in the Dominican Republic (1965) and Czechoslovakia (1968) confirm that the U.N. is equally unable to influence them. But not all political and diplomatic issues before the U.N. have the same intimate bearing on the vital interests of the superpowers as was claimed by them in the two cases just mentioned. The less the degree of vital interest involved the less, in proportion, will be the resistance of any countries concerned to such influences as may be generated in the U.N., and this general rule applies also to the superpowers.

Where is the line drawn beyond which these powers will bow to the will of the U.N. or be influenced by it in some measure? It clearly will not be permitted to infringe on any issue of national security, on their respective territorial spheres, and perhaps not even on matters that either superpower considers would seriously affect its image as it wants that image to be projected on the world stage. This last rather nebulous political area covers such matters as upholding of commitments to allies and friends. It is this area of possible intransigence that could have repercussions in Asia or in the Middle East— and possibly elsewhere—even though the geographical locations concerned are not within the generally accepted geographical limits of "reserved" territory. Yet, in the long run, intransigence in this area is not inevitable. Technological developments, internal changes in countries, altered international policies in various parts of the world all affect the foreign policy of the superpowers, as they do of other states. For example, foreign military bases are not of the same importance today as they were to both the superpowers ten years ago.

The point is that these fluctuations in the nebulous zone of interests do render the superpowers susceptible to the impact of the U.N. in certain situations. There have been cases in which the expression of massive U.N. opinion has had some effect on the political behavior of the superpowers. In the judgment of this writer, the United States has so far been more responsive to U.N. opinion than the U.S.S.R. Perhaps the most striking case occurred in the summer of 1958 after the United States landed a contingent of marines on the shores of Lebanon as a move to stem the growth of pro-Nasser forces in that country. This American action led directly to the convening of the Third Emergency Special Session of the U.N. General Assembly, an occasion that the United States regarded as of such high importance that President Eisenhower addressed the Assembly virtually as the chief delegate of his country. The President, facing the strong wave of feeling at the U.N. that the foreign forces sent to Lebanon should be withdrawn, made a six-point proposal. The clear implication was that this six-point proposal could be a good basis for withdrawal of the marines. The proposal was not accepted, except peripherally, and yet within a few weeks the United States, bowing to strong U.N. feeling in favor of most of the Arab states, voted for a resolution that made a rather different set of recommendations to calm the troubled area. That resolution, to which the United States had at first been cool, was adopted unanimously.[8]

There are fewer dramatic cases of U.N. influence on Soviet behavior, but there have been cases of proposals adumbrated by the Soviets in their opening statements at the General Assembly's annual general debate that have not been pressed because they failed to rouse enthusiasm among the general membership of the U.N. One significant instance occurred in April 1962 when the eight nonaligned members of the Eighteen-Nation Disarmament Committee worked out a proposal for a test ban. Informally the proposal was shown to the leaders of both the United States and Soviet delegations before it was presented to the Committee. The chief Soviet delegate, Valerian Zorin, found it completely unacceptable and attacked it fiercely—to put it mildly. However, the nonaligned countries decided to present their proposal anyway and did so. It was greeted by a sullen and much upset Zorin. Two days later the Soviet delegation received instructions from Moscow to accept the proposal as the basis of discussions for a test-ban treaty. Clearly, the Soviet authorities—it was understood that Khrushchev himself had so decreed—decided to respond to the united stand of the nonaligned world.[9]

Notwithstanding these instances, for the United States and the Soviet Union the U.N. is still a forum rather than a force. The questions that arise are, first, what categories of cases should, in their view, be brought to this forum, and second, whether there are differences in their policies in this regard.

Certain general rules of conduct emerge. One important one is that the worse the relationship between the two superpowers, the more competitive they become in their appeals to the U.N. forum. It follows that in the fifties, when the cold war was at its severest, there was a strong united front by the United States and its allies on the one side, and a considerable effort by the Soviet Union on the other side to gain the sympathy of the nonaligned countries by assiduous championing of the cause of decolonization, by assailing exploitation of various kinds, and by favoring their proposals in the field of disarmament. The United States' counterappeal to the nonaligned and developing countries was mainly in making by far the biggest contributions to the economic, technical, and children's programs of the U.N. This was not all the United States did. In 1958 it took a quiet and still generally unknown but nevertheless important initiative in regard to the racial policies of South Africa—which had already become a major political issue at the U.N. Until that year the United States would not vote for the U.N. resolutions on apartheid. At the 1958 General Assembly, the U.S. delegate to the Special Political Committee, to which the item had been assigned, sought out the Indian delegate and informally proposed that the two sit down together privately and see whether they could jointly work out the text of a draft resolution on apartheid that would be mutually acceptable. The Indian delegate agreed. From their effort emerged the first resolution on apartheid at the General Assembly that was affirmatively voted by the U.S. delegation. Before this result could be achieved, the Indian delegation, which had accepted responsibility for the draft resolution, had to convince the other Asian countries, the Arab states, the few independent African states then in the U.N., and a number of Latin American states that it was wise to accept the text that had been worked out with the U.S. delegation. This was accomplished, and the voting on the resolution marked a milestone in the history of the apartheid issue at the U.N.[10]

Thus, there have been moves and countermoves by the United States and the Soviet Union to gain good standing with the growing number of nonaligned and other newer delegations at the U.N. This is a delicately balanced game and often has to be played on the basis of instructions from the highest quarters of the two governments. Particularly in the sensitive field of disarmament, the two have tried to outbid each other, even though at times they have probably made their bids with reservations. For example, when Khrushchev, at the United Nations General Assembly in 1959, first advanced the dramatic formula of General and Complete Disarmament, U.S. officialdom was of two minds about agreeing to play at this seemingly utopian level. But in 1961 President Kennedy decided that politically it would be necessary for the United States to go along with a GCD approach, and he himself introduced the outlines of a plan for General and Complete Disarmament in his address to the General Assembly that year.[11]

The game of one-upmanship with regard to disarmament proposals has had the value of forcing the policy statements of the two governments toward convergence in some particulars. It is not yet by any means certain that the pressuring process has given a true indication of what the two sides would in fact accept: there have not been any substantive agreements to reduce armaments, or, indeed, even to eliminate the testing and developing of nuclear weapons. The 1963 limited test-ban treaty drove testing underground, at least on the part of the United States, the Soviet Union, and Great Britain. It has inhibited the testing of mammoth warheads, but only after most strategists had expressed a preference for smaller warheads. Besides, extrapolation from the results of underground tests can still lead to the manufacture and deployment of massive warheads. It is, then, prudent to say that the response of the superpowers to nonaligned pressures on disarmament issues—which was more a feature of the early 1960's than it is of the present time—stemmed primarily from initiatives exerted in various U.N. forums,[12] and probably remains to date more an exercise by the U.S.A. and the U.S.S.R. to acquire enhanced prestige in the U.N. world than to reveal bona fide shifts in fundamental positions which could lead to disarmament agreements.

It is true that the SALT talks appeared to make a promising beginning at Helsinki and that, at the time of writing (May 1970), several businesslike sessions have been held at Vienna. But these moves are very far from substantive agreements; they are certainly less promising than was the accord between the United States and the Soviet Union (September 1961) on the eight principles to govern negotiations on general and complete disarmament. The SALT talks, important as they are, are more limited in scope, which should conduce toward their chances of success. But there are other significant factors to be taken into account: old suspicions, the growing Chinese nuclear capabilities, unresolved sensitive situations such as those in South-East Asia and the Middle East, and an agglomeration of impeding internal factors in the two countries and within their governments.

Even if the SALT talks keep the pepper out, they are hardly likely to yield more than agreement on a system of signals which will increase mutual cognition between the U.S. and the U.S.S.R. as to the respective moves of these two states in regard to future development of nuclear armaments. This system could result in controlling and deescalating the nuclear arms race between them, but probably not actual disarmament. However any tangible gain will be worth achieving, particularly if it turns out to be a basis for a next round of talks aimed at substantive nuclear disarmament. The present round is hardly likely to persuade the nonnuclear states that Article 6 of the nonproliferation treaty has been complied with.

If this is a pessimistic view, it is at least backed by the evidence that there has not yet been a single weapon laid down

as a result of the protracted, involved, and often circular disarmament efforts that have gone on in and around the U.N.
since the beginning of 1946. It is conceivable that the apparent
shifts of position made by the United States and the U.S.S.R.
may in the future contribute toward the formulation of such
approaches as will be conducive to actual agreements. If this
view can be sustained by future developments, it will be possible to say with more assurance of the U.N. forum that though
it is not a force, and does not tangibly influence the superpowers
when their vital interests are concerned (and they themselves
are the sole judges of what their vital interests are), by stimulat-
ing the competitive instincts of the two superpowers it does
set up plays and patterns of behavior that could become the
basis of a new look at complicated international situations.

Allowing oneself a certain degree of optimism, it might be
said that the United Nations tends to encourage a certain
amount of healthy competition between the United States and
the U.S.S.R. before the eyes of much of the rest of the world.
The rules of the game are such that the superpowers have not
always been able to control the issues that come before the
UN: the Assembly by a majority vote and the Security Council
by a vote of nine members can put any item on the agendas
of these organs. The superpowers have adjusted themselves to
this situation. In the Security Council they have more control
over the discussion of issues, and on this body they have continuity; the others with continuity have been more or less willing
to go along with the lead of the United States. The remaining nine members are transients. They have a substantial disadvantage tactically. The game is played as the big two want it
to be played. When they fall out the Council becomes moribund.
For example, in June 1967 the U.S.S.R. abruptly decided that
it had had enough of the Council on the Middle East issue and
that it would have a better chance of gaining support for its
point of view in the Assembly. There was nothing the United
States could do about this situation, but accept it. This means
that the side that takes the initiative in the competition between
the superpowers has a certain tactical advantage—which does
not necessarily spell victory. The U.S.S.R. did not get what

it wanted from the Fifth Emergency Special Session of the Assembly (which it had asked for);[13] and neither did the United States get what it wanted out of the Second Emergency Special Session.[14]

Another aspect of the political behavior of the U.S.A. and the U.S.S.R. at the United Nations that has emerged in the post-cold war period of the middle and late sixties has been their tendency to take some advantage—and I use the phrase in a nonpejorative sense—of the readiness of the rest of the world to applaud agreements reached by them. The two acted on this basis in placing before the General Assembly, for its blessing which was duly forthcoming,[15] their joint statement of agreed principles for disarmament negotiations which they worked out in the summer of 1961. In 1963 the United States and the U.S.S.R. told the General Assembly that they would not station nuclear weapons and other weapons of mass destruction in outer space. Thereupon the General Assembly welcomed this agreement between the two superpowers, introduced a draft resolution on the subject, and adopted it by acclamation.[16] Then again, on December 19, 1966, the General Assembly unanimously commended the treaty on the peaceful uses of outer space that the United States and the U.S.S.R. had negotiated.[17]

The readiness with which the General Assembly and other U.N. bodies have welcomed agreements between the superpowers encourages the conversion of these agreements into multilateral treaties and this is all to the good. But there are indications that the members of the U.N. are going to be more circumspect about agreements between the two leading powers, and that it cannot be assumed, as seems to have been the tendency on the part of the United States and the Soviet Union, that their agreements with each other will always be automatically endorsed by the membership of the U.N. Most of the members of the Eighteen-Nation Committee on Disarmament resent the manner in which certain agreements between the superpowers have been handed down. In this connection the revolt over their treaty on the nonproliferation of nuclear weapons, which will in the long run probably turn out to have been effective, is significant. The resolution introducing the treaty on nonproliferation was sponsored by the United States and the Soviet Union and by some of their friends. It was adopted by a comfortable majority.[18] But these bare facts are far from the whole story. More important was the unprecedented volume of dissatisfaction with a super-power agreement that was aired in a long debate on the draft treaty. Eighty-nine delegates spoke on the draft treaty. Among them was the delegate of Turkey—a country that has been among the most friendly and loyal to the United States of all the membership of the U.N. on matters concerning international security. Speaking nearly at the end of the debate, Ambassador Eralp of Turkey said that *"almost every speaker"* had indicated that "the treaty deviated rather sharply from the guide lines of Resolution 2028 (XX) which set forth, among other things, the equality of obligations between the nuclear and non-nuclear states." [19] Had there been a secret ballot vote, it is doubtful that the draft resolution would have obtained the requisite two-thirds majority. As it was, as many as twenty-five states did not vote for the resolution and a few absented themselves at the time of the vote.

In 1969–1970 the superpowers suffered a clearer reverse at the U.N. This was in regard to their draft treaty on the pro-hibition of the emplacement of nuclear weapons and other weapons of mass destruction on the sea-bed. In October 1969 the United States and the U.S.S.R. presented a draft treaty on the subject to the Conference of the Committee on Disarmament (CCD). Most of the nonaligned states regarded the treaty as inadequate in the light of its proposed objectives. The super-powers made some inconsequential changes in their draft, and placed it again unsuccessfully before the Conference. Hoping to sway the General Assembly to their support, they then placed it before the twenty-fourth session of the Assembly. But they met with no success. The General Assembly asked the CCD—in effect the two superpowers—to reconsider the draft (GA resolution 2602 F. XXIV dated 16 December 1969). This was a significant parliamentary reverse for the two superpowers. On reconsideration of the matter at the CCD in March–April 1970, the superpowers made some further minor amendments to their proposed treaty. These too failed to render the draft acceptable to the nonaligned, and the U.S.S.R. and the United States, acting as cochairmen of the Conference, proposed an early vacation for that body. The superpowers must now either make more substantive concessions to the nonaligned or decide to enter into a bilateral arrangement in regard to their mutually agreed but not universally acceptable guidelines.

Now that, so far as the superpowers are concerned, the competitive character of the U.N. forum is being mitigated to some degree, there is, as we have seen, more than a mere possibility that the United States and the U.S.S.R. will run into trouble when their policies, if not coinciding, at times proceed on parallel lines. The resulting mirror-image appearance of the two rouses some suspicion that what is now shaping up might turn out to have more in common with the 1815 concept of a world at peace and in order than with the 1945 concept that was injected into the U.N. Charter.

How important to the world and to the superpowers is the current disaffection with the U.N. which is related to a certain degree of disillusion with the policies and behavior of the two superpowers?

The crux of the answer would appear to lie in the fact that for the United States and the Soviet Union the U.N. is not central either to their policies or to their concept of behavior as world powers. If this appears to be a strong statement, let us recall that so centrally located and well-informed a scholar as Henry Kissinger does not even once mention the U.N. in his latest book on American foreign policy, and this although the publishers tell us that the book examines "the prospects for international order in an era of high international tension." [20] It is surely striking that in examining the prospects today of international order there should be no mention whatsoever of the leading international organization of the era, and one that the United States was instrumental in creating.

This is not a one-sided phenomenon. The comprehensive and authoritative Soviet publication, *Fundamentals of Marxism-Leninism*, does not mention the United Nations in its section on the "Possibilities for Preventing War in Our Time." [21] In discussing "Basic Principles of Peace Policy" there is passing mention of the U.N. as the forum in which the U.S.S.R. put forward its proposal for general and complete disarmament,[22] and I believe there is no other mention of the U.N. in the whole manual which runs to over seven hundred pages.

On the highest governmental level, there was no mention of the U.N. in President Nixon's inaugural address. On the Soviet side the situation is similar. Soon after twice visiting the U.N. and creating, in his way, quite an impression there, Mr. Khrushchev made a marathonic speech on October 17, 1961, to the 22nd Congress of the Communist Party of the Soviet Union. The first part of this report dealt with the world situation and the international position of the Soviet Union. This part alone extended to some 16,000 words but in it there is only one brief paragraph on the U.N.—on changes in its machinery and on equal representation in its organs for the three groups of states in the world.[23] And when Mr. Khrushchev summed up "the tasks which the present international situation raises for Soviet Foreign Policy," he made no mention whatsover of the U.N.[24] In this respect at least, his successors are all Khrushchevites.

Although neither the United States nor the Soviet Union regards the United Nations as central to its foreign policy purposes, I suspect that there are American and Soviet policymakers who find the U.N. useful. In this there is perhaps a measure of hope for the international community, but any viable concept of world order must be closer to the 1945 compromise formula than to an institutionalization of a great-power condominium.

NOTES

1. For text see *Year Book of the United Nations*, 1946–1947, p. 2.
2. Article 26 of the U.N. Charter.
3. State of the Union Address by President John F. Kennedy, January 30, 1961.
4. *New Times*, No. 26 (June 30, 1969), p. 26.
5. The next day, July 31, 1969, at the 424th meeting of the Eighteen-Nation Disarmament Committee (as it continued for a time to be called), a number of delegates made brief, restrained "diplomatic" statements to place on record mild versions of the views

they had expressed on the previous day. See ENDC/PV. 424 dated July 31, 1969.

6. General Assembly Resolution 1(I) of January 24, 1946.
7. The status of cochairmen for the foreign ministers of the United States and the Soviet Union was proposed in informal discussions by India just before the commencement of the first ENDC's meetings in March 1962. It was quickly espoused by Canada and strongly canvassed by India and Canada. It was accepted—at the time rather reluctantly—by the superpowers.
8. For a fuller treatment see Arthur Lall, *Modern International Negotiation* (New York: Columbia University Press, 1966) pp. 76–79.
9. The text of the proposal of the eight nonaligned members of the ENDC, which has since been revived in a slightly modified form by Sweden, is to be found in document ENDC/26 dated April 16, 1962.
10. This is a summary of the relevant events. It is, I believe, accurate. The two principal delegates concerned were George Mc-Gregor Harrison for the United States and myself for India. The culmination of the draft we drew up was G.A. Resolution No. 1248 (XIII) dated October 30, 1958.
11. U.S. Arms Control and Disarmament Agency, *Documents on Disarmament, 1961*, pp. 465–482.
12. For the reasons previously set out, I include the Eighteen-Nation Disarmament Committee (ENDC) in this group.
13. The emergency session of the General Assembly called in June 1967, on the initiative of the U.S.S.R., dealt with the Middle East crisis.
14. The emergency General Assembly session called in November 1956, on the initiative of the United States, dealt with the Hungarian situation.
15. G.A. Resolution No. 1722(XVI) dated December 20, 1961.
16. G.A. Resolution No. 1884(XVIII), October 17, 1963.
17. G.A. Resolution No. 2222(XXI), December 19, 1966.
18. G.A. Resolution No. 2373(XXII), June 12, 1968.
19. U.N. document A/C. 1/PV. 1578, June 4, 1968, p. 16.
20. Henry A. Kissinger, *American Foreign Policy* (New York: Norton and Company, 1969).
21. *Fundamentals of Marxism-Leninism*, 2nd rev. ed. (Moscow: Foreign Languages Publishing House, 1963), pp. 464–469.
22. *Ibid.*, p. 473.
23. *Documents of the 22nd Congress of the CPSU*, Vol. 1 (New York: Cross Currents Press, 1961), p. 55.
24. *Ibid.*, p. 62.

DECOLONIZATION *

Harold Karan Jacobson

I

Decolonization has been one of the most important developments in international relations during the quarter century
following World War II. In these years roughly a quarter of
the world's population gained independence as political sovereignty was transferred from the metropolitan countries, mainly
located in Europe, to new (at least in terms of the twentieth
century) states, mainly located in Asia and Africa. As a consequence, the nature of the international system has been profoundly altered. On the most elementary level, the number of
political units in the system has more than doubled. More
fundamentally, to the extent that gaining sovereignty can be
equated with enfranchisement, the voice of the Southern Hemisphere in the international system has been vastly amplified.

The United Nations has been deeply involved in the process of decolonization. Of course, the extent of its involvement
has varied from case to case. Clearly it has hardly ever been
the sole or even the principal determinant of the course of
action. Nevertheless, issues concerning decolonization have constantly been on the agenda of the world body. Debate in the

* This chapter is based on work done under the auspices of the International
Organization Program, The University of Michigan. I wish to express my gratitude
to David and Margaret Karns for their assistance in the preparation of the statistical
material used here.

U.N. has reflected and affected the broad process of decolonization, and on several occasions U.N. organs have played important roles in both crises and routine events and have had a significant impact on the outcome. The process of decolonization has also affected the United Nations, for its nature as a political institution has changed as the new states have swelled its ranks.

A process with such profound consequences as decolonization could hardly have been ignored by the two principal powers in the international system, the Soviet Union and the United States; on the contrary, they have both been deeply interested in it. The United States itself had colonies, and thus, even had it wanted to, could not have avoided entanglement. More important, since American decolonization has been a relatively minor part of the process, both the Soviet Union and the United States have acted as if they believed that decolonization could have substantial implications for their interests.

In most instances neither the Soviet Union nor the United States has been directly involved in the process of decolonization other than through their membership in the United Nations; therefore, the world organization has been an important vehicle for their policies concerning these issues. Frequently, of course, they have each simultaneously pursued policies outside the U.N., but the U.N. has given them a legitimate and natural access to issues which they otherwise would not have had and which has been important to them. Given their standing as the two most powerful members of the international system during this period and their consequent status in the U.N., these two states have inevitably affected the course that the organization has pursued. Furthermore, each in its own way and at varying times has sought to shape this course through initiatives.

If the number of people still under colonial rule were the sole factor determining what place the issue of decolonization would have in the future of the United Nations, an analysis of Soviet and American policies concerning these matters would be mainly of historical interest, for, even ignoring the effects of population growth, less than one-twentieth of the number who had colonial status in 1945 had it still in 1970. But other factors than numbers are important, and these point to decolonization's being a prominent concern of the United Nations for some years to come.

The largest and most populous of the remaining dependent territories are in the southern third of Africa, where minority white regimes seem determined to retain control. Moreover, the fate of these territories has become inseparably linked with that of apartheid and the existing regime in South Africa, which is even more uncompromising. The other dependent territories are largely the oddments of empire—islands and enclaves. What independence would mean for them is far from clear. Sovereignty over some of them is contested, and several of them have traditionally been regarded as having military significance; thus their decolonization also is not likely to be easy. Whatever the resistance, representatives of the new states who now compose a majority of the United Nations membership, seem committed to continue to press for decolonization. Given these facts and forces the future salience of decolonization in the U.N. is assured.

Undoubtedly the U.N.'s activities in this field in the seventies will be different from those of the preceding quarter century, but some carry-over can be expected. Many of the issues that will have to be faced have already been broached, and over the years the policies of the major participants in the process of decolonization, including those of the U.S.S.R. and the United States, have demonstrated marked continuity. Thus the record of the past, to which we now turn, is not only of interest in itself, but also as a precursor of the future.

II

In 1945 neither the Soviet Union nor the United States could accurately be characterized as a supporter of the colonial *status quo*. So far as colonialism writ large was concerned—that is, the principal possessions of the European powers in Asia and Africa—both superpowers seemed to assume that it was a fading phenomenon, and the United States was already committed to granting independence to its largest and most populous dependency, the Philippine Islands. This general outlook, however, did not prevent either the Soviet Union or the United States from acquiring territorial spoils in the manner typical of victors in war. The United States gained control of the Marshall, Caroline, and Mariana Islands, and also of the Ryukyus, including Okinawa. The Soviet Union obtained the Kurile Islands and regained the southern part of Sakhalin and the adjacent islands. In addition, it obtained possession by lease of Port Arthur and Dairen and rights to the operation of the Chinese-Eastern Railroad and the South-Manchurian Railroad, the latter providing an outlet to Dairen. In an earlier era these acts might well have been labeled imperialism, but in 1945 hardly a voice was raised to so malign the victors, and in terms of the total colonial situation, these acquisitions were indeed minor. Their impact on the broad views of the two superpowers toward this situation was limited in the case of the United States and nonexistent in that of the U.S.S.R.

The prospective role for the United Nations concerning colonialism as envisaged in the Charter, like so many parts of that document, was very much a product of American planning. The origins of Chapters XI, XII, and XIII of the Charter, dealing with non-self-governing territories and the Trusteeship System, can all be traced to papers drafted in the Department of State. While the proposals were modified in the process of gaining general acceptance, the final version of the Charter was acceptable to the United States and, more than that, accurately reflected the American view of how colonial issues should be handled in the postwar period.

This view foresaw and favored decolonization, but assumed that it would be a gradual process. The end result for the colonies would be various forms of self-government, independence being but one variant. Meanwhile, international institutions would be evolved to oversee colonial administration and to promote the application of humane and progressive policies. Given American ideas on the time span that would be involved in decolonization, notions concerning international supervision of colonial administration assumed a central role in the overall scheme. However, the United States felt able to impose only limited obligations on the colonial powers and it was of a mixed mind about the obligations that it would itself accept. What the United States sought to insure was an orderly and peaceful transition, and one that would not jeopardize long-run Western economic and political interests. Indeed, it assumed that decolonization was a way of insuring the security of these interests.

The Soviet Union, understandably in view of its prewar experience and war-time situation, had given much less attention to planning postwar institutions. Initial Soviet views can be suggested by the title of the document in which they were embodied, "Memorandum on the International Security Organization." In this concept, colonial issues would have been of concern to the future organization only when they involved serious disputes. Nevertheless, the U.S.S.R. soon accepted the broader mandate envisaged in the American plans, including the Trusteeship System. This was a significant development, for even as a member of the League of Nations the Soviet Union had condemned the Mandates System on which American plans essentially were based.

The amendments that the U.S.S.R. submitted at the San Francisco Conference were designed to underscore the principle of self-determination and the objective of independence.[1] They also aimed at insuring that the U.S.S.R. would have a rightful voice in the Trusteeship System—specifically, that it would have a seat on the Trusteeship Council and would be involved in the negotiation of the Trusteeship Agreements. It won the first point but not the second. Other Soviet proposals, which were completely unsuccessful, would have increased the authority of international institutions. One would have provided that strategic areas, which under the Trusteeship System are accorded special treatment, should be designated on the recommendation of the Security Council, instead of leaving the matter to the administering authority, as was the practical effect of the provision that was adopted. The Soviet Union also suggested that the United Nations should designate the countries that would administer the Trust Territories.[2]

The general Soviet posture was best summarized by Molotov at a press conference held during the San Francisco meetings when he said, "We must first of all see to it that dependent countries are enabled as soon as possible to take the path of national independence." [3] In sum, the Soviet Union sought to lay claim to a position in the vanguard of the anticolonial movement. It further sought to insure that it would have a voice in the handling of colonial issues within the United Nations.

The U.S.S.R. also had other ambitions. In September 1945 in London at the First Session of the Council of Foreign Ministers, the Soviet Union pressed a claim to become the administering authority for a trusteeship to be established in the former Italian colony of Tripolitania, a claim that met immediate and sharp resistance from the United Kingdom and the United States.[4] The disagreement persisted for three years until eventually the problem was transferred to the General Assembly which in 1949 decided that Libya including Tripolitania should not be a Trust Territory, but rather become independent by 1952.

What expectations the Soviet Union had about the fate of its claim, and how seriously it took it, cannot be known. The rhetoric that Molotov used when he first advanced the claim alluded to Soviet privileges in Dairen and Port Arthur and asserted that the U.S.S.R. should also have bases in the Mediterranean for its merchant fleet. Had the Soviet claim been accepted, it surely would have been a windfall for the U.S.S.R., for in contrast to the United States, which became the Administering Authority of the former Japanese Mandate of the Marshalls, the Carolinas, and the Marianas only after it had captured and occupied the islands at great human and material costs, the U.S.S.R.'s troops were never near Tripolitania.

The fact that the Soviet Union desired to advance this claim may have been a factor in its acceptance of the Trusteeship System with so little criticism, for even though the concept of the System was substantially different from that of the Mandate System—and more anticolonial in orientation, with the requirement that the Trusteeship Council be composed of equal numbers of administering and nonadministering states—the Trusteeship System was hardly designed to impose stringent requirements upon the administering authorities. In any case, the Soviet Union appeared not to take the system too seriously, and it boycotted the first two sessions of the Trusteeship Council on the ground that the Trusteeship Agreements had been negotiated in an unconstitutional manner since the U.S.S.R. had not been involved.

Perhaps at this early stage in the United Nations the most significant difference between the Soviet Union and the United States was in their attitude toward the Trusteeship System. Both were anticolonial—to be sure, the U.S.S.R. was the more so, both favored the broad involvement of the U.N. in colonial issues, but both also had their own territorial ambitions which they wished to pursue in a relatively unfettered manner. With respect to the colonies of others, the Soviet Union appeared to want a platform from which to urge their rapid liquidation, the United States an instrument to oversee an orderly transition. Each could read the U.N.'s mandate as being suited to its own interests.

III

The policies that the Soviet Union and the United States first enunciated concerning the U.N.'s role with respect to colonial issues during these early days were pursued with remarkable constancy in the years that followed. But as the years went by, the colonial situation changed and so did the United Nations. Because of these changes the quarter century from 1945 through 1970 falls rather naturally into three periods: 1945–1955; 1956–1959; and 1960–1970. During the first decade the decolonization that occurred was concentrated mainly in Asia and the Middle East and the membership of the United Nations was relatively stable. The second period was a transitional phase. After the Bandung Conference in 1955, the anticolonial movement became increasingly militant; decolonization in Africa gained momentum; and in December 1955 a record number of states gained membership in the United Nations, boosting the total from sixty to seventy-six. The year 1960 saw the decolonization of a substantial part of Africa, and in consequence again a record number of states gained admission to the U.N., so that the membership jumped from eighty-two to ninety-nine. These changes in membership were to have crucially important effects on the politics of the General Assembly.

During the early years of the first period, the Soviet Union pushed harder in some ways for the involvement of the U.N. in colonial issues than did the United States. It was the Ukrainian Soviet Socialist Republic that in January 1946 raised the Indonesian issue in the Security Council. By the same token, during the discussion of the possible modalities for implementing the vague obligations of Chapter XI of the Charter, which applied to dependent territories generally, the Soviet Union sought to establish for them a regime equal to the Trusteeship System with its right of petition and visiting missions, rather than something much milder, as the colonial powers desired. Despite or because of its initiatives, the Soviet Union increasingly came to be excluded from the U.N.'s work (as opposed to its public debates) concerning colonialism. It played no role in the U.N.'s mediatory efforts in the Indonesian crisis; it was not put on visiting missions to the Trust Territories or *ad hoc* committees; and its proposals seldom became the basis for U.N. activities.

Perhaps because of this exclusion over the years, the U.S.S.R.'s enthusiasm for the U.N.'s involvement in colonial issues waned. However, the Soviet Union did not go so far as to attempt to block efforts to have the U.N. dampen and ameliorate post-colonial conflicts in the Middle East and the Indian subcontinent. It refrained from exercising its veto in the Security Council, even though the West would have predominant influence in implementing the resolutions that were adopted and their effect would be to ease the Western predicament in choosing sides between rival parties in these areas.

In contrast, during the years from 1945 through 1955, the United States was deeply involved in everything that the United Nations did concerning colonialism. American representatives were key figures in the Indonesian situation, and American proposals frequently guided the work of the Trusteeship Council and the Committee on Information from Non-Self-Governing Territories. From the American point of view, involving U.N. organs in the sticky situations in the Middle East and the Indian subcontinent was the best approach for tackling agonizing and seemingly insoluble problems.

There were also similarities in the positions adopted by the two superpowers. Neither listed the islands adjacent to Japan that they had acquired or gained control of at the end of World War II as being territories for which they had an obligation to transmit information to the United Nations under the provisions of Chapter XI of the Charter. The United States did, however, place the Marshall, Caroline, and Mariana Islands (which had been a Japanese mandate) in the Trusteeship System, though it declared the entire territory to be a strategic area and thus assured itself the protection of its veto by making the Security Council ultimately responsible for the supervision of the trusteeship. Finally, neither the Soviet Union nor the United States sought to bring the deteriorating situation in Indochina before the United Nations.

The second period, the years 1956 through 1959, was one of transition. Decolonization, largely completed in the Middle East, began in Africa, as the Sudan, Morocco, Tunisia, Ghana, and Guinea became independent. The U.N.'s supervisory activities continued with the Soviet Union and the United States playing their by now customary roles, the former that of the principled critic and the latter, the progressive administering authority.

The Suez crisis, triggered by the Anglo-French and Israeli attack on Egypt, was the most dramatic episode on the U.N.'s agenda during this period. It also brought forth a rather unusual response by the U.S.S.R. In a letter to President Eisenhower, Nikolai Bulganin, Chairman of the Council of Ministers, after referring to Soviet and American naval and air forces in the Mediterranean, proposed that the two governments "join their forces in the United Nations for the adoption of decisive measures to put an end to the aggression." [5] The United States lost no time in rebuffing this proposal, preferring instead U.N. action less pointedly directed against its allies and friends and involving military forces from states other than the great powers. Since France and the United Kingdom used their right of veto to prevent the Security Council from acting, the resolution authorizing the creation of the United Nations Emergency Force was adopted in the General Assembly under the provisions of the Uniting for Peace Resolution. The United States strongly supported this procedure; in contrast the U.S.S.R. assailed it as violating the Charter. While important, this difference between the superpowers should not obscure the fact that both wanted the U.N. to take some action to prevent steps by Britain and France that might have resulted in reestablishing colonial control in the Middle East.

The year of African independence was 1960; of the seventeen new states that joined the U.N. that year, sixteen were located on the African continent. The entrance of these new states decisively tipped the balance in the General Assembly in favor of anticolonialism. In his celebrated stint as Chairman of the U.S.S.R.'s delegation to the Fifteenth Session of the General Assembly, Nikita Khrushchev sought to capitalize on this development. In his first speech to the Assembly he proposed that the United Nations adopt a declaration on the granting of independence to colonial countries and peoples. Although the African and Asian states ultimately preferred their own version of the declaration, the Soviet Union could claim credit for initiating the resolution that emerged, 1514 (XV). African leaders would subsequently hail this resolution as being "as important to Africa as the Charter of the United Nations and the Universal Declaration of Human Rights."[6] The United States, along with Australia, Belgium, the Dominican Republic, France, Portugal, Spain, South Africa, and the United Kingdom, abstained in the voting on this resolution. All the other eighty-nine members of the UN that were present voted for it.

The following year, the U.S.S.R. proposed that a body be created to oversee the implementation of Resolution 1514 (XV), and while the African and Asian states again preferred their own draft, the proposal was adopted. This time the United States was included among the ninety-seven that voted for the resolution. The Soviet Union supported this committee's right to receive petitions from individuals in dependent territories and to dispatch visiting missions to the territories.

Meanwhile, the Congo crisis had developed and was running

its course. Both the Soviet Union and the United States voted for the Security Council resolution that created the United Nations Force, but they did so for quite different reasons that were openly expressed. The Soviet representative interpreted the principal purpose of the resolution to be "to ensure the immediate and unconditional withdrawal of the Belgian troops." [7] The United States representative, on the other hand, felt that its primary purpose was to restore and preserve order in the Congo.[8] Eventually, the U.N.'s involvement in the Congo contributed to both goals, but in the process most observers agree that the outcome favored Western interests and not those of the U.S.S.R.[9] As in so many of the U.N.'s operational activities, while the Soviet Union was largely excluded from what went on, the United States played a central role. The U.S.S.R. bitterly protested the situation, and frequently cited the Congo operation as something that the U.N. should not repeat.

Nevertheless, it did not seek to block the establishment of another U.N. Force designed to promote order in a conflictive aftermath of colonialism in Cyprus.

As the sixties wore on, and the U.N.'s involvement in the Congo was brought to a close, attention in the world body increasingly focused on the remaining problems of decolonization: the Portuguese colonies, particularly Angola and Mozambique; Southern Rhodesia; South West Africa; apartheid in South Africa (which the Africans saw as an extension of colonialism); and the oddments of empire.

By 1970, with its jurisdiction reduced to New Guinea and the Trust Territory of the Pacific Islands, and its membership to Australia and the United States as administering authorities and China, France, the U.S.S.R. and the United Kingdom as nonadministering authorities, the Trusteeship Council had virtually faded into oblivion. The Committee established to oversee the implementation of Assembly Resolution 1514 (XV), formally known as the Special Committee on the Situation with Regard to the Implementation of the Declaration on the Granting of Independence to Colonial Countries and Peoples, and informally as the Special Committee of Twenty-four (of Seventeen from 1961 through 1962), asserted its jurisdiction over all remaining colonial territories, and this body and its creator, the General Assembly, became the focal points of all U.N. hortatory activities concerning colonialism.

Increasingly militant, the Africans and Asians pressed the initiative in these two bodies, with support and encouragement from the U.S.S.R. The United States, on the other hand, more and more found itself the target of criticisms—its investments and military assistance allegedly lending support to racist regimes —and called upon to undertake actions against these regimes which it would not. The Africans became so militant in fact that at the close of the U.N.'s first quarter century, the problems of Southern Africa came close to dominating the attention of the General Assembly. Despite this changed context, the U.S.S.R.'s position was little different from what it had been in 1945—it was still committed to rapid decolonization; that of the United States, however, seemed to have shifted in a conservative direction.

IV

In 1945 both the Soviet Union and the United States had regarded decolonization not only as inevitable, but also as desirable, and both favored the U.N.'s involvement in the process. In the twenty-five years that followed, they continued to share these broad general assumptions, and as the record has demonstrated, their policies generally were based on them. But within this framework of agreement, other assumptions held by the two superpowers were different and even contradictory.

Although the United States was certain in 1945 that decolonization was inevitable, it thought that the process would be much more lengthy than it has been. While the time span envisaged by the United States was repeatedly foreshortened as the years went on, at least until 1960 it never fully adjusted to the rapidity with which the colonial situation changed. Soviet expectations concerning timing have always been less explicit, but the U.S.S.R. seems not to have been quite so surprised as the United States was about the pace of decolonization. On the contrary, many of its efforts aimed at accelerating the process.

More fundamental differences between the assumptions held by the two superpowers relate to why they considered decolonization desirable. From a doctrinal point of view, both the Soviet Union and the United States saw decolonization as being instrumental to maximizing human welfare. For the Soviet Union, however, decolonization was but one step in the historical progression toward socialism, while for the United States decolonization was preeminently a political issue with hardly any economic implications. To the extent that the doctrines of either dealt with ultimate outcomes, for the Soviet Union decolonization would eventually lead to a world socialist state. For the United States, in contrast, decolonization would contribute to a vaguely defined world order based on cooperation among states each constituted according to the principle of self-determination.

On a more immediate level the Soviet Union saw decolonization as a way of diminishing Western influence throughout the world. Colonial disputes would cause difficulties for Western governments, and once a colony was granted independence the former metropole's capacity to order matters in the territory would be greatly reduced. The U.S.S.R. also saw some opportunity to gain influence in the new states, although its optimism on this score has fluctuated significantly during the past quarter century.

American views about the immediate benefits of decolonization were sharply opposed to these. The United States saw decolonization as a foresighted means of preserving Western influence in the Southern Hemisphere; as the cold war developed, timely decolonization was a favorite American prescription for preventing the growth of communism. To a limited extent the United States also saw decolonization as a means of gaining economic access to territories from which it had been barred under the colonial regime, but this was far from the most important factor shaping American policy.

The underlying reason for the two superpowers' favoring the involvement of the United Nations in the process of decolonization was that it was a way of insuring that they themselves would be involved: a way of gaining legitimacy for their advice and their claims for a voice in disputes. Consistent with these assumptions, both the Soviet Union and the United States

have favored giving the United Nations substantial authority over
colonial territories, and the U.S.S.R. has gone even further in
this respect than the United States. In part, the United States'
caution and unwillingness to accept Soviet proposals along these
lines can be explained by the fact that it also saw the United
Nations as a device for controlling and limiting Soviet influence.
Thus, despite its proclivities, it could not favor increasing the
authority of the United Nations if this might carry with it additional opportunities for Soviet influence.

The United States saw the United Nations' involvement in
the process of decolonization as a means of managing the transition in orderly fashion: of easing the inevitable tensions and controlling the crises. The United States often saw the U.N. as the
most effective instrument for intervening in conflicts arising in
the immediate aftermath of colonialism and dampening them.
Since decolonization went on within the Western and not within
the socialist world, the Soviet Union did not share these concerns
to the same extent. On the contrary, in its view the prime function
of the U.N. was to hasten rather than manage the process of decolonization, nor could it accept the American belief that the
U.N. should limit Soviet influence. At the same time, however,
the U.S.S.R. generally preferred U.N. to Western intervention
in postcolonial conflicts. At least when the operations were conducted under the U.N. the Soviet Union had some claim to a
voice, whereas the situation was seldom such that Western intervention would surely fail and provoke a reaction sharp enough
to give the field to the U.S.S.R. The Soviet Union might have
preferred to intervene by itself, but that was rarely a viable
option, and moreover might have carried a substantial risk of
direct military clashes with Western countries, particularly the
United States—something the U.S.S.R. has generally sought to
avoid.

The objectives that the Soviet Union and the United States
have pursued have been intimately related to these assumptions.
The way in which these objectives have been given concrete formulation and the success that the two superpowers have had in
gaining them can be seen to a certain extent in the historical

account above. This view can now be amplified by a more analytic treatment.

For purposes of analysis it is possible to distinguish three levels at which objectives might be defined and success in achieving them measured. The first is the level of the parliamentary situation in the United Nations; that is, to consider the U.N. as a forum where resolutions are proposed and put to vote. The second level involves the activities conducted by the United Nations or in its name. And the third level involves the actual situation in the colonies and former colonies.

If each state's initiatives were contained solely in resolutions that it alone sponsored and these were voted on without alteration, the percentage of these resolutions that were adopted would be a good indicator of that state's success in the parliamentary situation. Unfortunately, these conditions are seldom met. The sponsors—and multiple sponsorship is frequently the case— may or may not be the original authors of a resolution, and as debate in the U.N. progresses changes in proposals are frequent. Moreover, the objectives of both the Soviet Union and the United States have not been confined to getting their own proposals adopted, but have been much broader. In general terms, both have sought widespread support for their positions and to be part of the mainstream of the U.N. Thus voting on any proposals with the winning side (*yes* when the resolution is adopted and *no* when it is not) is a more appropriate criterion than the number of its own proposals that are adopted.

Table 1 gives scores for the Soviet Union and the United States—in terms of voting with the winning side on colonial issues—for the three periods used in the historical account above. As can be seen, although the two started out in roughly the same position, voting with the winning side slightly more than half of the time, their success moved dramatically in different directions as the U.N. developed. A partial explanation is that as new states have joined the U.N. the balance of forces has shifted increasingly toward the anticolonial side. U.N. resolutions have become more radical, and while the Soviet Union could accept these, the United States could not. The issues under consideration have also changed, and those considered in the last period have affected the United States much more directly than those considered in the earlier periods. On the level of the parliamentary situation then, the picture has been one of increasing Soviet and decreasing American success.

Table 1

VOTING WITH THE WINNING SIDE *

	1946–1955	1956–1959	1960–1967
Soviet Union	55%	63%	83%
United States	56%	51%	36%

Shifting from the resolutions that the United Nations has adopted to the operations that it has undertaken, the score as revealed by the historical account is much more favorable to the United States. The U.N. has seldom taken action of which the United States seriously disapproved, but it has gone against Soviet wishes frequently. Here the simplest explanation is probably also the most important. The United States has provided the bulk of the financial support for the U.N.'s operational activities. The explanation favored by the Soviet Union is that Western nationals have had disproportionate influence in the U.N. Secretariat, and no doubt the fact that they have had more influence than nationals of socialist states has had an effect on what has been done.

It is too early to tell which side will enjoy greatest success with respect to influence in the new states, for what is at issue is a long-run historical process. In view of the limited Soviet influence prior to 1945 in colonies in Africa and Asia, it can be argued that the U.S.S.R. has made impressive inroads. On the

* These percentages are calculated on the basis of all roll call votes in the General Assembly on colonial issues as defined by the author occurring during the years cited. A listing of these votes is available on request. There were 483 votes in the first period, 205 in the second, and 332 in the third. It might be argued that some account should be taken of abstentions, and if that is done and the measure is *not voting against the winning side* (voting *yes* or abstaining when the resolution is adopted and voting *no* or abstaining when it is not) the results are indeed different. For the Soviet Union the figures calculated for the three periods are respectively: 69%, 73%, and 90%; and for the United States, 70%, 74%, and 69%. Since one is hardly part of the mainstream when one abstains, however, the more rigid measure was chosen for Table 1.

other hand, the expectations advanced by Soviet writers in the late fifties and early sixties about the rapid alignment of the new states with the socialist world have been found uniformly over-optimistic on any issues other than those concerning further decolonization.[10] The United States experience with new states has not always been pleasant either, and in the late sixties both superpowers appeared to be somewhat disillusioned with the results of decolonization.

Several factors other than the broad assumptions held by the Soviet Union and the United States have also been important in shaping their policies on decolonization in the United Nations, and these factors are related to the differential successes. First, the United States has been more directly subject to the United Nations' activities than the Soviet Union. This is because American colonial holdings as traditionally defined were initially more extensive than the U.S.S.R.'s as has also been American trade with states in the southern part of Africa. Second, in the cold war the United States has been allied with the colonial powers, and none of these with the possible exception of New Zealand has been as convinced as the United States of the inevitability or desirability of decolonization. Finally, because the United States objective has been to retain Western influence in new states while that of the Soviet Union has been to displace it, the United States has had to be much more concerned than the U.S.S.R. about an orderly transition. As a consequence of these factors the United States has been subject to many more cross pressures than the Soviet Union. The American Government has usually been divided within itself about the posture that it should take on colonial issues, and the advice and pleading from its allies has more often than not run counter to its own anti-colonial instincts and the demands of the colonial peoples. It is significant, however, that these cross pressures have restrained the United States considerably more on the declaratory level of the parliamentary situation in the U.N. than they have with respect to the institution's operational activities.

The Soviet Union has been subjected to cross pressures too. There has been an inherent conflict between its objective of displacing Western influence and its desire to avoid direct military clashes with Western countries and particularly the United States. Furthermore, as its quarrel with Communist China has developed, it has continually run the risk of being outflanked in its anticolonial position. These cross pressures have had virtually no effect on the Soviet Union's declaratory policies which have been consistently extreme. They may well, however, have affected the Soviet Union's ability to collaborate with the U.N. in dampening postcolonial conflicts.

In a sense the policies of each of the superpowers have been a spur to the other to be more anticolonial. The effect of their combined policies has been to insure that the United Nations would be deeply involved in the process of decolonization and that as an institution it would come down on the anticolonial side. The net result is undoubtedly to have hastened the process of decolonization and probably to have made it more peaceful.

V

Trying to draw implications for the future from the past is always hazardous, and it is particularly so in this case, in which a variety of vaguely defined variables interact in only dimly seen ways and in a context that is changing. Nevertheless, there seems to be no reason why prevailing patterns in the U.N.'s declaratory activities should not be projected for some time into the future. For the past few years the African-Asian majority in the United Nations has with Soviet support demanded increasingly stringent measures to bring colonialism to a close in the southern part of Africa and also steps to terminate quickly the colonial status of the remnants of empire. The West, including the United States, which would bear the burden of applying the measures designed to liberate Southern Africa, has been unwilling, and it has regarded the problems with respect to the oddments of empire as complicated ones that should not be hurried; thus, the United States' decline in voting with the winning side.

The dynamics of the situation are such as to work for its

perpetuation. For the Soviet Union to become less anticolonial would make it vulnerable to the charges of Communist China. Beyond that, the U.N.'s declaratory activities embarrass the West at very little if any cost to the U.S.S.R. Nor can the new states of Africa and Asia back down very easily. To do so would deny the rhetoric which they have used among other things to cement the solidarity of their group. An anticolonial posture in the U.N. can also have certain domestic payoffs. It can be used to keep alive in the postcolonial period the *élan* that was such a vital part of the struggle for independence. Also not to be anticolonial risks domestic and external criticism. Nor can the West be expected suddenly to accept the anticolonial demands. To do so would involve costs far more substantial than opprobrium in the United Nations.

But will matters develop beyond the declaratory level? Specifically, will the Soviet Union be willing to provide the necessary sinews to give effect to the African and Asian demands? Will it take the place traditionally occupied by the United States as the principal supporter of the U.N.'s operational activities? If the past record is any guide, negative answers are appropriate for all of these questions.

To pose possible scenarios, the U.S.S.R. conceivably could agree to support a force authorized by the General Assembly under the Uniting for Peace Resolution with the purpose of implementing the 1966 decision revoking the mandate for South West Africa, or Namibia as this territory is now called in the General Assembly, from South Africa or of toppling the current regime in Rhodesia (Zimbabwe). Such scenarios, however, seem most unlikely to be realized. In all of the discussions of the situation in Southern Africa, while fully backing the demands of the Africans and Asians, Soviet delegates have constantly adhered to the U.S.S.R.'s well-known position that decisions to employ enforcement measures must be taken within the framework of the Security Council. Thus they have insisted that the decisions be subject to veto by the United States, China, France, and the United Kingdom, as well as by the U.S.S.R. For all practical purposes, given the attitude of the Western powers, this means that such decisions will not be taken. To go the route of the Uniting for Peace Resolution would violate the Soviet Union's firm position concerning how the U.N. should operate.

Furthermore, to support such an operation would increase substantially the Soviet Union's contribution to the U.N., and it has been noticeably niggardly over the years. Then too, supporting such an operation would risk confrontation with the United States, which the Soviet Union seems to desire to avoid. In addition, given the U.S.S.R.'s distrust of the U.N. Secretariat, it would see little gain to giving this body a free hand in a liberated area. Finally, the record of Soviet attempts to gain influence in new states would probably suggest to Soviet policy makers that their efforts would at best bring problematic results.

Thus there seems to be little reason for the Soviet Union's going beyond its present position. Nor have African and Asian states overtly suggested that it should. On the contrary, they have been much more interested in bringing pressure on the Western powers than they have been in forming an alliance with the U.S.S.R. for operational purposes, and judged by their own domestic actions, many of these states seem to fear substantial active Soviet involvement.

The U.N.'s activities in the field of decolonization in the early seventies then will most likely look very much as they did in the late sixties: characterized by acrimony, talk, and strident resolutions. The situation would change if the West, and particularly the United States, acquiesced in the demands of the Africans and Asians and took forceful measures to liquidate colonialism in Southern Africa. Whether or not Western initiatives might reorient the U.N.'s activities in this field is moot. Conceivably they could, but given the dynamics of the present situation it would be difficult. In any case, there has been little indication that such initiatives will be forthcoming. But the key to change is surely in the hands of the West, and again particularly of the United States.

NOTES

1. See Ruth B. Russell, assisted by Jeannette E. Muther, *A History of the United Nations Charter* (Washington, D.C.: The Brookings Institution, 1958), pp. 808–842.
2. United Nations Conference on International Organization, *Documents* (New York, 1945), Vol. X, p. 441.
3. *The New York Times,* May 8, 1945, p. 15.
4. James F. Byrnes, *Speaking Frankly* (New York: Harper & Row, Publishers, 1947), pp. 94–97.
5. Paul E. Zinner, ed., *Documents on American Foreign Relations, 1956* (New York: Harper & Row, Publishers, 1957), p. 356.
6. Alex Quaison-Sackey, *Africa Unbound: Reflections of an African Statesman* (New York: Frederick A. Praeger, Inc., 1963), p. 139.
7. United Nations, Security Council, *Official Records* (873rd Meeting, July 13–14, 1960), p. 43.
8. *Ibid.*
9. See for example Ernest W. Lefever, *Uncertain Mandate: Politics of the U.N. Congo Operation* (Baltimore: The Johns Hopkins Press, 1967).
10. For a quantitative index, see Edward T. Rowe, "Changing Patterns in the Voting Success of Member States in the United Nations General Assembly," *International Organization,* Vol. XXIII, No. 2 (Spring 1969), pp. 231–253.

ECONOMIC DEVELOPMENT: THE GREAT POWERS AND THE SEA BED *

Daniel S. Cheever

More than 70 per cent of the earth's surface is covered by the world ocean, and most of that area is beyond the limits of national jurisdiction. Because technology has made available this area's rich natural resources, its governance has become a matter of international concern. In 1967, for example, Malta urged the U.N. General Assembly to take measures to demilitarize the ocean floor "beyond the limits of present national jurisdiction and to internationalize its resources in the interest of mankind." Her spokesman, Ambassador Pardo, urged the "creation of an international agency . . . to assume jurisdiction as a trustee for all countries over the sea-bed and the ocean floor underlying the seas beyond the limits to present national jurisdiction." [1]

Under these circumstances, the temptation to speculate on the interplay between the exploitation of sea-bed resources and the superpowers' attitudes with respect to the United Nations is irresistible. Will the increased use of deep ocean resources provide new opportunities for the United Nations? Will technological advance in ocean resource exploitation boost the stock of the functionalists who argue that the way to build world order is to concentrate on practical economic and social problems rather than political matters? Or, will the increased use

* The research assistance of Miss Margaret Galey and Mr. Michael Houlahan is gratefully acknowledged.

of ocean and sea-bed resources lead one to conclude, in John Stoessinger's phrase, that "the functionalist thesis [should] be inverted"? [2]

The Soviet Union and the United States will play major roles in determining the fate of the Maltese proposal. They are the world's leaders in marine science and technology. Both are sufficiently predominant in naval strength and underwater technology to defy any regulations an international agency might seek to enforce against their wishes. Equally important, they are leaders in the rival East–West blocs at the U.N. At the same time, they are the most prominent industrially advanced nations in the North–South confrontation with the developing countries. Both have exhibited considerable sensitivity to many questions raised by the Maltese proposal including arms control, economic aid, freedom of scientific inquiry, and the degree of independence appropriate for international agencies.

To gauge the possible effects of sea-bed developments on the U.N. this paper seeks first to examine Soviet and American behavior in U. N. economic organizations over the past twenty-five years. Second, the positions of the Soviet Union and the United States on certain issues in the ocean debate are compared. Finally, on the basis of these considerations, some projections are made about the future role of the U.N. in regulating the use of the sea bed.

On the basis of this approach, a tentative conclusion emerges: Due largely to parallel Soviet and American interests, no major change in the role of the U.N. in fostering economic development is in store as a consequence of man's capacity to intensify his exploitation of ocean space and sea-bed resources. The two major industrial powers will continue to hold international agencies on a short rein.

A CONGRUENCE OF INTERESTS

The Soviet Union and the United States are often thought to hold the U.N. in fundamentally different perspectives. The former has been described as ideologically antagonistic to international organizations; the latter has been held to be in favor of them. This difference in perspective is thought to be greatest in international economic relations, and stems in all probability from initial and largely continuing Soviet disinterest in the Economic and Social Council and the Specialized Agencies. While this proposition is valid generally speaking, it cannot be taken to mean that the two superpowers are inevitably on the opposite sides of the international organization fence. Both governments tend to back international agencies when they enjoy majority support. Both employ such agencies when it seems possible to further their national goals by doing so. Both powers, in short, seem more pragmatic than ideological in their approach to international organization.

Alvin Z. Rubinstein reached a similar conclusion six years ago when he noted that the two governments behaved similarly in coping with U.N. economic and social activities. Both opposed any significant expansion of large-scale operational responsibilities. Both were held to be inordinately preoccupied with parliamentary victories, thereby politicizing economic issues to the detriment of constructive achievement. Both governments were found to be chary of large-scale fund-raising activity or the expansion of executive authority, especially when their views were in the minority. The result was a congruence of behavior thought to limit the effectiveness of U.N. economic and social organizations in meeting the needs of developing countries. A further broadening of the areas of congruence was warned against as implying "profound and disastrous significance for the future of these organizations." [3]

Does this proposition hold true five years later? Or will the two powers take a more permissive view of the U.N. as they consider the implications of growing capacities and needs to utilize sea-bed resources? Will they stand together if other governments seek to strengthen international agencies as a means of protecting their interests in ocean resources? Their behavior will do much to determine the answers for two principal reasons.

First, the Soviet Union and the United States are the only major naval powers in the world today. This state of affairs is startling because it is relatively novel. Although Germany,

Japan, and, to a lesser extent, France were eliminated as naval powers during World War II, British naval power has only recently receded from the shores of empire. As it did so, the United States Navy was at first unrivaled. Now the Soviet Union is developing a nuclear submarine fleet allegedly capable of significantly compromising American deterrent capacity partially sea-borne in missile-carrying nuclear submarines. The Soviets, moreover, are thought to have a strategy that makes the most of their inferior surface fleet by closing off strategic waterways controlling the approaches to their shores, and by mobilizing considerable naval strength in such strategic areas as the Eastern Mediterranean.[4]

Inevitably both governments are concerned to protect their naval power, particularly their undersea capacities, when considering the establishment of regimes (including rules and institutions) to promote ocean resource exploitation. In this respect there is a difference between *coastal nations,* of which there are approximately one hundred and seven, and *maritime powers* of which there are only two. The proficiency of the Soviet Union and the United States in ocean technology in combination with industrial strength and nuclear capacity accentuates the military bipolarity that has characterized world politics since 1945. This is not because the Soviet Union equals the United States in naval strength, or is likely to do so for some time to come, but because Soviet land-based missiles are counterbalanced in some degree by American sea-based missiles which are effective as a deterrent largely because they can be deployed secretly at sea.

Second, the Soviet Union and the United States are the world's major oceanographic powers. As such they tend to be predominant in the peaceful use of ocean space much as they are in outer space. Many of the world's leading oceanographers and marine scientists are Soviet and American citizens. The success of international programs such as the International Decade of Ocean Exploration (IDOE), initiated in the U.N. by the United States in support of a Long-Range Expanded Program of Ocean Research (LEPOR), will depend heavily on Soviet and American efforts.

The Soviet capacity in marine science affairs has been recognized in the U.N. and the Specialized Agencies. No longer does the Soviet Union lack decision-making power in all U.N. secretariats as it did five years ago.[5] From 1963 to 1969 a Soviet citizen, K. N. Federov, served concurrently as head of UNESCO's Office of Oceanography, and as Secretary of the Intergovernmental Oceanographic Commission (IOC) established in 1960 as a semiautonomous body with UNESCO. Significantly, he succeeded an American, Dr. Warren Wooster, in these posts. Moscow, what is more, was the site of the last International Oceanographic Conference held in 1966. The two World Data Centers, established in support of the International Geophysical Year (IGY) of 1958, are located in Moscow and Washington. These centers are important for collaborative ocean investigation such as the recent International Indian Ocean Expedition (IIOE) and the forthcoming International Decade of Ocean Exploration.

Soviet and American citizens have been prominent in the Special Committee on Oceanic Research (SCOR) of the nongovernmental International Council of Scientific Unions (ICSU). The Soviets participate in several fishery commissions and rank fourth in terms of annual fish catches. Although not yet a member of FAO, Soviet experts nonetheless serve on that agency's Advisory Committee on Marine Resources Research (ACMRR) which for marine science affairs links FAO with UNESCO, the World Meteorological Organization (WMO), and SCOR. Thus, the past decade has witnessed the recognition in the U.N. of the Soviet Union's coming of age as an oceanographic power.

Trade and Aid

Both governments are influenced in their attitudes toward international economic organizations by the behavior of the numerous developing countries. Although at first wholly uninterested if not opposed to U.N. economic and social organization, for example, the Soviet Union, finding itself disadvantageously isolated from the Third World, made an important policy re-versal in 1953 by announcing its willingness to contribute funds to the Expanded Program of Technical Assistance (EPTA).[6]

Both the United States and the Soviet Union at first opposed the establishment of a capital development fund, a project close to the heart of nonaligned developing countries as early as 1951. By 1955, however, the Soviet Union changed sides having won two important conditions: (a) the proposed fund should make loans rather than grants; and (b) it should be entirely separate from the IBRD (World Bank) in which Soviet bloc states do not participate.

The United States continued to oppose the capital development fund proposal. It held out against the Special United Nations Fund for Economic Development, SUNFED, but as a palliative promoted the establishment of the International Finance Corporation in 1956 to assist developing countries through private investment. Finding this step inadequate to assuage the feelings of nonaligned countries and to prevent the Soviets from capitalizing on the popularity of the SUNFED proposal, the United States next proposed a "special projects fund." To make this project acceptable to Congress and the American electorate, vital compromises were struck. The new fund was not to be a "development fund" but rather an assistance agency engaged in preinvestment natural-resource surveys, industrial research, and manpower development.[7] On this basis, the United States could and did contribute funds without altering its opposition to SUNFED. As a consequence, the new Special Fund commenced operations on January 1, 1959. By 1965, it was combined with EPTA to form the U.N. Development Program (UNDP) and remains under the leadership of an American, Paul Hoffman.

At this juncture it would appear that the developing countries were enabled to make progress in establishing international economic agencies because the major power blocs were competing for their favors. Their success was limited. When they finally succeeded in getting the General Assembly in 1966 to establish a U.N. Capital Development Fund, structured on the model of the UNDP but intended to distribute grants and soft loans, the United States voted in the negative, and the Soviet

Union and its allies abstained despite earlier indications of support. The first pledging conference of October 1967 was even more ominous. Neither of the two powers would open its pocketbook. Because it seemed ridiculous to set up a moribund agency, the UNDP was asked to assume responsibility for the paltry sum scraped together by a few of the more conscientious and less destitute developing countries.[8]

Considering the popularity of the stillborn fund among the developing countries and the opportunity to diminish its own economic isolation, it may seem surprising the Soviet Union failed to support it. The United States, confronted with Vietnam, civil disorder, and congressional antipathy, was in no mood to compete. The new organization might have been held up by the Soviets as a rival to the IBRD-IDA "capitalist" complex. The Soviet Union's behavior suggests that its initial concern was to curry favor with the developing countries. When the day of reckoning came, however, it was loath to be the only potential donor in the agency.

The behavior of the United States is more understandable. The only economic programs the United States supports are those established on its terms such as the UNDP and, more particularly, those it can largely control, like the World Bank, through weighted voting and other procedural or organizational devices. The U.N. Capital Development Fund does not meet these qualifications.

While both governments attack projects not to their political taste, the United States seems more intransigent. While the Soviet Union opposed U.N. projects in South Korea, Taiwan, and South Vietnam, the United States exerted even greater pressure, though unsuccessfully, on the UNDP to block a minor technical-assistance project for Cuba.[9] Both by-pass international agencies by resorting heavily to bilateral aid rather than multilateral aid. There seems little chance, therefore, that the United States will accept a recommendation of the Commission on Marine Science, Engineering and Development (Stratton Commission) that would seek to establish an international fund to receive and distribute a share of the profits derived from sea-bed resources beyond recommended limits of national jurisdiction.[10]

If such a proposal is to be acceptable to the United States and the Soviet Union, it will be for reasons that have little to do with their present and past attitudes toward international economic organizations.

This skepticism is fortified by the record of Soviet and American contributions to U.N. development-assistance programs, a ready indication of their relative support of multilateral aid efforts. Although the Soviet record lags behind the American effort, neither government goes very far down the multilateral road. The annual Soviet contribution to the UNDP and its predecessors (EPTA and the Special Fund) remained at $3.6 million from 1961 through 1967, while annual U.S. contributions doubled in the same period to reach a total of $70 million in 1967. As a result, the Soviet share of the total has decreased from 4 to 2 per cent compared to a steady U.S. 40 per cent. This record, incidentally, has little to do with these governments' "capacity to pay." The regular U.N. budget is assessed on this principle and draws 32 per cent of its total from the United States and 17 per cent from the Soviet Union.[11]

Another comparison of United States and Soviet multilateral aid is afforded by their annual voluntary contributions to *all* international agencies engaged in international aid giving. The United States executive in FY 1968 requested $140.9 million for voluntary contributions to twelve programs including the UNDP. The Soviet Union plus Byelorussia and the Ukraine in calendar year 1967 contributed to only four of these programs for a total of $4.8 million including the UNDP. What is more significant for the prospects of establishing an aid dispensing ocean agency is the proportion of its total aid each donor lays on the multilateral line. In 1966 U.S. multilateral contributions represented just over 3 per cent of its total economic aid to developing countries, while the Soviet multilateral effort amounted to about one-half of 1 per cent of its total program.[12] Both donors, like the great majority of donors for that matter, rely predominantly on bilateral economic assistance.

The UNCTAD (U.N. Conference on Trade and Development) experience provides an analogy which is helpful in projecting the politics of exploiting sea-bed resources in that it illustrates the saliency of the North–South confrontation in economic matters. At both UNCTAD I and II the less developed countries were clearly discontent with the *status quo* in international trade. They sought to alter cherished principles of the GATT system which they claimed served the interests of the major, developed trading nations for which free trade and mutual tariff reduction provided tangible benefits. Similarly, many developing countries resent the *status quo* on the sea bed. The current international regime governing the exploitation of seabed and sub-seabed resources favors the rich. That is, under the 1958 Convention on the Continental Shelf a coastal state's capacity to exploit resources effectively determines the limits to its jurisdiction. No depth today is beyond technology's reach, and economic feasibility tends to extend seaward with technological advance. In developing countries' perspectives, the present international regime regulating sea-bed resource exploitation, like the GATT regime, threatens to widen rather than narrow the income gap between rich and poor.

In U.N. debates on the sea-bed issue several members have asserted that developing countries should receive preferential treatment in the distribution of economic benefits from resources beyond the limits of national jurisdiction. At UNCTAD I, however, the United States and its allies opposed most of the majority demands including preferential treatment for developing-country exports, measures to counter fluctuations and long-term declines in the terms of trade for primary products, and proposals for a new trade organization to be concerned specifically with these matters. The United States, indeed, initially opposed even the convening of the Conference. As a consequence of its behavior, the "U.S. became clearly identified as the least willing of the industrialized countries to even consider a new international division of labor which would permit the developing countries to industrialize." [13] The American voting record on the General and Special Principles of the Final Act adopted at UNCTAD I was the most negative at the conference.[14]

While the Soviet Union, on the other hand, stood with the majority on 26 out of 28 votes, it was less than successful in asserting that the difficulties of developing countries were due solely to the nefarious Western bloc. The U.S.S.R. denied the significance of the alleged North–South split, maintaining that the East–West division was responsible for the world's economic as well as its political ills. Although sympathizing with developing-country grievances, the U.S.S.R. bade them direct their complaints to the Western countries alleged to have exploited them as colonies in the past and as neocolonies since their independence. The U.S.S.R. denied any responsibility for obstructing trade in commodities and manufactures. Yet she was unable to reach full agreement with the UNCTAD Seventy-Seven on the wisdom of a new trade organization to replace the GATT, expressing more concern than they for expanding East–West trade and less concern for North–South trade.

Neither the Soviet Union nor the United States, however, has remained wholly unresponsive to the pressures exerted by developing countries in the UNCTAD forum. The Soviets in January 1965 announced the removal of all external tariffs on developing countries' primary products. While this would have been a dramatic step for the United States to take, in the case of the U.S.S.R. it was practically meaningless because external tariffs are not a major factor in determining commodity prices, which are controlled internally instead. Nor were the less developed countries pleased to be told that the best way to increase their exports to the Soviet Union would be to increase their imports from that country.[15]

By UNCTAD II the United States, in turn, had softened its position somewhat. At the Punta del Este Conference of the Heads of American States in April 1967, President Johnson announced a willingness to explore the possibility of granting temporary preferential tariff advantages to all developing countries in the markets of all industrialized countries, a step hailed by the UNCTAD Secretary-General as an important gain. This statement was followed up by an announcement by the United States in UNCTAD II at New Delhi in 1968 that tariff preferences to all less developed countries without reciprocity on their part was accepted in principle by the United States and all UNCTAD States.[16]

The UNCTAD experience, in sum, suggests that while the

U.S. and the U.S.S.R. have not been wholly unresponsive to the development demands of the Third World, they resist the establishment of agencies that threaten to increase the political leverage of developing countries. This attitude is resented by the UNCTAD majority which continues to demonstrate in matters of trade and development the solidity of the North–South confrontation. The countries of the East were included with the West in the South's attack on the North. Cold war polemics between East and West at the first Conference were denounced as irrelevant to the problems raised at Geneva by the "Third World" countries.[17] It is hard to avoid concluding from this record that the Soviet Union and the United States will be reluctant to entrust any sea-bed resource to which they may feel entitled by virtue of their industrial technology to an international agency for the benefit of poor nations.

International Inspection

In urging a new sea-bed regime, Ambassador Pardo was as much if not more concerned to prevent nuclear conflict as he was anxious to insure an equitable distribution of economic benefits. The title of his long agenda item for the twenty-second session of the General Assembly was "Examination of the question of the *reservation exclusively for peaceful purposes* of the sea bed and the ocean floor and the subsoil thereof, underlying the high seas beyond the limits of present national jurisdiction, and the use of their resources in the interests of mankind."[18] The Assembly's response suggests this concern was shared widely. It established without dissent an Ad Hoc Committee to study various aspects of the agenda item. This committee, after honoring its instruction to report to the next Assembly, was succeeded by a permanent committee—the Committee on the *Peaceful Uses* of the Sea Bed and the Ocean Floor Beyond the Limits of National Jurisdiction.[19] Although the United States, the U.S.S.R., their allies, and the nonaligned powers in the Sea-bed Committee seemed to agree on the principle of limiting the uses of the sea bed to peaceful purposes, there is a question whether they can agree on the arms control measures that may be necessary to put it into practice.

Precedent for workable international inspection is by no means lacking. Three types of inspection techniques are in operation currently. In the first type each party assures itself of the behavior of its own nationals and enterprises and is able also to "inspect" or monitor to its satisfaction the activities of the other parties. Examples of this type are found in the arrangements provided for in the Test Ban and Outer Space Treaties. Indeed, these came into force very largely because they did *not* require *international* inspection. A second type, probably more relevant for the sea-bed situation, is mutual inspection by *national* teams. The Antarctic Treaty of 1959, for example, authorizes inspection of any area on the continent by national teams to insure compliance with the treaty's ban on military uses. This procedure has proved acceptable to date. The third type involves inspection by *international officials*. An example is afforded by the statute of the International Atomic Energy Agency authorizing inspection of national nuclear plants by teams of international civil servants as elements of an on-going inspectorate to ensure that nuclear-assistance projects are used solely for peaceful purposes.[20] Both the Soviet Union and the United States have participated in these control arrangements.

Whether one of the three types or modifications thereof will be necessary to ensure that the sea bed beyond national jurisdiction will be used "exclusively for peaceful purposes" depends in large degree on technical considerations beyond this discussion's scope. Already the Stratton Commission, in recommending that an International Registry Authority be established as a control element in a new international sea-bed regime—with the power to inspect all stations, installations, equipment, and other devices used in operations under internationally registered claims, has implied that the IAEA and its policies afford a possible model for the sea bed. The Commission to Study the Organization of Peace has also alluded, in its 19th Report, to the IAEA as a possible model for the sea bed.[21]

The United States' and U.S.S.R.'s past experience in IAEA

may be revealing with respect to international inspection of the sea bed. The United States took the initiative for the IAEA in 1953 as part of President Eisenhower's Atoms For Peace program. In that year and the year following, the Soviet Union rejected six different American memoranda dealing with the program's implementation on the grounds that prohibition of nuclear weapons would have to precede the creation of an Atoms For Peace agency. It agreed that discussion of the peaceful uses of atomic energy should be separated from disarmament and took an active interest in the drafting of an international statute only when the United States threatened to go ahead without it. An initial eight-nation drafting group of Western atomic powers was expanded accordingly to twelve to include Brazil, Czechoslovakia, the U.S.S.R., and India. The latter had echoed the Soviets' dismay at the small size of the original group and had urged further that the General Assembly, representative of all nations, should play a role in sponsoring and approving the treaty. The Indian delegate found ready support for his views among Third World delegates. Oceanographic, mineral, and other interests in the United States, be it noted parenthetically, are skeptical of any major role for the Assembly in either establishing or supervising a new sea-bed regime.

Although organizational issues were difficult to resolve, the negotiating group came up with a unanimous set of recommendations, including a traditional tripartite structure of an international operating agency. It was to have a board of governors, a general conference, and an administrative staff headed by a director-general. In one interpretation of events, agreement was possible because the superpowers "had a joint interest as atomic producing powers that gave them a closer understanding with each other on certain issues than with the atomic 'have-nots'." [22] In some respects the politics of ocean resources are similar.

More difficult to decide was the composition of the board and the relationship among the three organs. On this issue the U.S.S.R. was tempted to forsake the United States for the have-nots. At first the United States and the U.S.S.R. were in agreement on a sixteen-member board, dubbed an "Atomic Security Council," that was attacked by India, speaking for a large majority of atomic have-nots, as having too much authority. The Soviet Union promptly switched sides to favor a larger board. A new round of negotiations produced a twenty-three member board selected on the basis of a complex set of compromises. The top five atomic powers are assigned to what amount to permanent seats. These powers, in turn, co-opt the leading atomic power in each of five remaining geographic areas. Two countries are selected as producers of source materials on an annual basis. One country is designated on an annual voting basis as a supplier of technical assistance. Finally, ten members are elected to the Board annually by the entire membership of the general conference. With those changes the U.S.S.R. rejoined the U.S.A. in support of the new draft.[23]

Equally revealing for sea-bed problems was the difficulty in agreeing on, and using, the IAEA inspection system. This resulted at first in what Stoessinger has called a "superpower by-pass" whereby IAEA inspection was ignored by both the major atomic powers in preference for far looser bilateral assistance agreements. While the Soviet Union seems to have led the way in debasing the Agency's inspection standards, the United States followed closely behind because Congress was unready to follow the Executive's policy of transferring fissionable materials to an organization in which communist states participated. The U.S.S.R. went so far as to enter into ten bilateral agreements with no inspection requirements whatsoever. In 1959, the United States in its turn, made fissionable material available to the EURATOM countries which insisted on their own inspection system. Not until June 1963 did the U.S.S.R. reverse direction and agree to the principle of Agency safeguards. The following year the United States went further and offered to place *all* of its agreements under Agency control.

These developments plus the inspection role assigned to it in the Nonproliferation Treaty seem to brighten the Agency's shaky start. What is significant here is that the Agency has established what amounts to an international corps of arms-control inspectors. Another point worth pondering is that after backing and filling the Soviet Union came down on the side of international authority—or at least approached the Western view of international organization—probably because of its concern to prevent the spread of nuclear weapons to potentially hostile nations, notably the Federal Republic of Germany.

The U.S.S.R. also appeared to have a similar interest in restraining American military activity on the ocean floor. The Soviet Union, for example, seemed determined to deny the United States the use of the sea bed for *any* military purposes. It submitted a draft resolution to the Ad Hoc Committee requiring all states to "use the sea-bed and ocean floor beyond the limits of the *territorial waters* of coastal states exclusively for peaceful purposes." [24] This differed sharply with the United States which urged instead "a workable, verifiable and effective international agreement which would prevent the use of this new environment for the emplacement of weapons of mass destruction." [25] Both agreed along with other members, however, that the question of arms limitation should be referred to the Eighteen-Nation Disarmament Committee (ENDC). In the discussions of arms limitations in the ENDC, now the Twenty-Six Nation Disarmament Commission, the United States and U.S.S.R. have developed similar views. The United States and the U.S.S.R. jointly submitted a draft treaty prohibiting the use or emplacement of weapons of mass destruction on the sea bed and, without specifying details, providing for a system of verification and control to be carried out without interfering with states' peaceful activities on the sea bed. This draft treaty was submitted to the 1969 General Assembly. There it failed to receive the Assembly's endorsement and was returned to the Disarmament Committee for further discussion. Significantly, the Assembly's failure to endorse the U.S.-U.S.S.R. treaty was a consequence of the small powers' efforts to force more stringent arms-control measures on the nuclear powers.[26] From these events, it appears that the two superpowers found it easier to agree with each other than with the nonnuclear powers.

A SEA-BED REGIME

The Maltese proposal boils down to two issues: Where are the limits to "present national jurisdiction"? What should be the nature of the "regime" beyond such jurisdiction?

These questions arise because of rapid advances in science and technology which have opened up a sea-bed frontier for those countries able to exploit it. The politics of these issues parallel the politics of international economics—especially trade and aid. Third World countries are interested principally in getting what they consider their fair share of the global patrimony. The oceans, beyond what traditionally have been modestly defined national limits, have heretofore belonged to no one, and their resources have been *res communis* for those countries able to exploit them. Developing countries are well aware that in the future the technologically advanced countries have certain advantages in exploiting ocean resources. While the superpowers and usually their allies tend to view the ocean floor in the perspective of East versus West, the developing countries, as at UNCTAD I and II, see it as North versus South. Because the latter division tends to predominate in the U.N., where the poor heavily outnumber the rich, the U.S.A. and the U.S.S.R. often find themselves herded into the same corner when international agencies are suggested as a means of promoting developing-country interests. A considerable similarity of views could be seen in the events attending the establishment of the Committee on the Peaceful Uses of the Sea Bed and the Ocean Floor Beyond the Limits of National Jurisdiction.

A New Sea-Bed Committee

The General Assembly took its most important action to date to deal with the Maltese intervention when, on the last day of its twenty-third session, it established a forty-two nation Sea-Bed Committee. The constituent resolution, number 2467A, one of a group of four, was adopted by the General Assembly on December

21, 1968, by a vote of 112 to 0 with 7 abstentions.[27] The two major powers diverged on this issue but not sharply. While not initially a cosponsor of the proposal introduced by Belgium, the United States became so subsequently and voted with the majority. The United States itself had proposed a sea-bed committee the year before on the model of the Outer Space Committee, a suggestion at once opposed by the U.S.S.R. In 1968 the Soviet Union abstained, an action consistent with its opposition to the creation of a new international institution to assume responsibility for sea-bed or sub-sea-bed resources as proposed in the Malta Proposal the year before. In opposing a new institution, the U.S.S.R. indicated that in an ideologically riven world international organizations must be held on a tight rein. They were in reality wolves in sheep's clothing. International cooperation would break down if control over sea-bed resources were turned over to "imperialist monopolies." [28]

On the other hand, some international organizations suit the Soviet Union. In discussing the sea-bed problem it played up the International Oceanographic Commission (IOC) while denigrating other U.N. bodies, including the Assembly. In the 1967 discussions of the First Committee, for example, it opposed the creation of the Ad Hoc Committee, the Sea-Bed Committee's predecessor, on the ground that such a step was premature until more was learned about the sea bed through IOC-sponsored investigation.[29]

This attitude is hardly surprising in view of what Marshall Shulman has described as an "exceptionally good" Soviet record in international scientific cooperation and what Dallin has noted regarding Soviet participation in "innocent agencies." [30] The Soviet Union has also become cooperative in fishing matters as noted above. She is not yet a party to the Geneva Fishing Convention, however, although she has signed the three other closely related conventions dealing with the Law of the Sea. The United States also backs the IOC and participates in fishery commissions.

On the particular matter of the new Sea-Bed Committee, the U.S.S.R. evidently did not feel strongly enough, or was not able, to bring all its allies into line. She was joined by Hungary, the Byelorussian S.S.R., and the Ukrainian S.S.R., along with Cambodia, Equatorial Guinea, and Cuba. But Bulgaria, Czechoslovakia, Poland, and Rumania parted company to support and cosponsor the proposal.

The second resolution, 2467B, dealing with pollution, presented no political problems. Introduced by Iceland, it was cosponsored by the U.S.A. and U.S.S.R. along with many other governments and of the four resolutions received the widest support in a plenary vote of 119 to 0 with no abstentions.[31]

The third resolution, 2467C, the only really controversial one of the four, could not be settled by consensus. It requested the Secretary-General to study and report on the question of establishing "appropriate international machinery for the promotion of the exploration and exploitation of the resources of [the sea-bed beyond national jurisdiction], and the use of these resources in the interest of mankind." The controversy was less East–West between the Soviet Union and the United States than it was North–South between a majority of the developing countries and a majority of the advanced countries. There were important exceptions among the advanced countries, however, including the Netherlands, Denmark, Norway, Sweden, and Japan. Introduced by Thailand, it was cosponsored first by three Latin American countries—Brazil, Ecuador, and Peru, plus Libya, the U.A.R., and Yugoslavia. These were joined subsequently by thirty-two other developing countries. The resolution was opposed vigorously by the entire Eastern European bloc and Mongolia and resisted by several abstainers including the United States, France, Italy, and the United Kingdom. The First Committee vote was 77 to 9 against with 18 abstentions. The plenary session vote was 85 to 9 against with 25 abstentions.[32]

While these votes reflect long-standing differences between the Soviet Union and the United States, they also show some congruence of interests. The Soviet Union and its allies have consistently sought to downgrade the office of the U.N. Secretary-General. This resolution brings him to the center of the stage. While the wealthier Western countries have backed the Secretary-General's office, they were reluctant in this case to single out one aspect of the sea-bed problem for special treatment by the Secretariat when the new committee itself was expected to look at the problem. In contrast, the Scandinavian countries and the Netherlands, in supporting the developing-country proposal, could have been emphasizing the importance they attach to international organization in their dealings with developing countries, including peacekeeping forces and multilateral sponsorship of development assistance. In the perspective of many developing countries, international executive authority may be important to protect their sea-bed interests. Accordingly, they endorsed the initiative requested of the Secretary-General. Confronted with a North–South issue, in short, the Soviet Union and the United States did not differ as sharply as might have been expected.

The fourth resolution, number 2467D, was adopted by consensus in the same plenary session. It was introduced by the United States and dealt with the desirability of an International Decade of Ocean Exploration (IDOE) to be undertaken within the framework of a long-term program of research and exploration "under the aegis of the United Nations." [33] It at once attracted favorable comment from the U.S.S.R. which took the opportunity to indicate the potential importance of the IOC in coordinating Decade programs and activities. On this issue the interests of the two major oceanographic powers are clearly congruent. As noted earlier, both are concerned to elicit cooperation with each other, with other advanced states, and with *all* coastal states, developed or not, in order to explore resources in, and gain knowledge of, the ocean depths. Both are concerned to protect freedom of scientific inquiry which, as a practical matter, means access to continental shelves, "adjacent" coastal areas, and even territorial waters. Both the United States and the Soviet Union see the IOC as an instrument to elicit this cooperation and to establish norms to promote oceanographic investigation.

Limits to Present National Jurisdiction

This question is one element of the Sea-Bed Committee's primary task of studying the "elaboration of legal principles and norms for promoting international cooperation in the exploration and use of the areas beyond national jurisdiction." It has become urgent rather suddenly because only within a decade have marine science and technology enabled man to use the deep ocean for military and nonmilitary uses alike. An effort was made in 1958 to deal with the emerging problems of jurisdiction and title when the Geneva Convention on the Continental Shelf limited coastal states' jurisdiction to the resources *on* or *under the shelf itself.* Beyond territorial waters, the oceans above the shelf retained their traditional common-use status as "high seas."

It was widely assumed in 1958 that the extent of national jurisdiction over sea-bed resources would not extend beyond a depth of 200 meters on the "adjacent" continental shelf. Article I, however, which defines the shelf, provides another definition in an "elastic" clause extending the shelf "beyond that limit, to where the depth of the superjacent waters admits the exploitation of natural resources of the said areas." Because no depth today exceeds man's reach, this exploitability clause no longer limits the shelf effectively. Because of economic constraints, however, several years may pass before even the most technologically advanced nations are able to conduct profitable operations beyond the 200-meter depth. Exploitation costs rise sharply as depths increase. Nevertheless, new discoveries of rich oil resources at great depths, in combination with technological breakthroughs, are tempting enough to give rise to claims of exclusive national jurisdiction far beyond present commercial operations which, for petroleum and gas, are still within the 200-meter isobath. Test drilling, however, is already routine at 300 meters and is feasible at 1,000 meters.

Underwater oil production on the shelves of twenty-two countries already amounts to 17 per cent of the world's total (about six million barrels per day) while 6 per cent of the world's natural gas production comes from offshore sources. Within ten years this total is expected to rise to 33 per cent of a world output of seventy million barrels a day.[34] Offshore petroleum development constitutes an increasing share of many countries' national economies and also brings in hundreds of millions of dollars in direct revenue to the government from the bonuses, rents and royalties from offshore petroleum concessions, and production.

In this situation, coastal states, whatever the stage of their technology and industrial development, are tempted to extend their claims of exclusive national jurisdiction far seaward to protect their future interests. What is more, there is a danger that rights of exclusive access for one purpose in the oceans, such as mineral exploitation on the sea beds, will "expand to claims of territorial sovereignty or exclusive access for all purposes. . . ." [35] This is alleged to have been the result of the Truman Proclamation of 1945 claiming for the United States sovereign rights over the natural resources of its geological continental shelf. Chile, Ecuador, and Peru each soon proclaimed its "sole sovereignty and jurisdiction over the areas of the sea adjacent to the coast of its own country and extending not less than two hundred nautical miles from the said coast." [36]

International boundaries in the oceans as well as on the ocean floor, in short, are in a state of flux. Claims over territorial waters range from 3 miles to 200 miles from shore. Exclusive fishery zones range from 12 miles to 200 miles. Exploration rights have been granted by governments many miles from shore in depths exceeding 500 meters. Some governments are uncertain what their claims should be. Nonetheless, all U.N. members who have expressed themselves on the subject, including the Soviet Union and the United States, agree in principle that there should be an "area" on the sea bed "beyond the limits of present national jurisdiction"; where and how large remain undefined.[37] Indeed, the principle in effect has gained acceptance by virtue of its inclusion in the Sea-Bed Committee's title.

Further evidence that the principle has gained wide acceptance is the fact that many governments in U.N. Committees have expressed dissatisfaction with the definition of national limits provided in the Continental Shelf Convention. Only two Ad Hoc Committee members, both Latin American countries, indicated that they were pleased with the definition. In addition, two other Latin American states and Australia, in saying that their particular claims were not up for discussion in the Committee, seemed to accept the present arrangements. The vast majority of representatives who spoke on the matter, including those from the Soviet Union and the United States, described the existing definition as inadequate. Both agree that the area beyond national jurisdiction needs a "precise boundary." Both, as has been noted, can be expected to resist extravagant national claims that might limit their rights of access to coastal areas for scientific investigation. In general, both feel their interests are served well by traditional freedoms on widely extended "high seas."

This congruence of views also holds for a "moratorium" on national claims to explore and exploit the area beyond national jurisdiction. In 1969 both the United States and the U.S.S.R. along with the Eastern and Western European blocs voted against Resolution 2574D calling for a moratorium on the exploitation of sea-bed resources pending the establishment of an international regime. The United States explained that the resolution rested on the "unsound and self-defeating premise" that technological capability for exploiting the sea bed should be retarded. The United States further stated that the "objective" is not for the Sea-Bed Committee to issue prohibitions against exploration but to ensure that any activities do not prejudice the solution of other activities.[38]

Moreover, the superpowers also voted against Resolution 2574A, which requested the Secretary-General to ascertain the views of member states on the desirability of convening a Conference on the Law of the Sea to define among other matters the limits of national jurisdiction over the sea bed. The vote in the Assembly was 65 in favor to 12 against with 30 abstentions.[39] The United States, in voting against the resolution, explained that law-of-the-sea questions must be considered in "manageable packages." Merging the question of national jurisdiction with other law-of-the-sea questions in a single conference would delay agreement on all sea-bed issues indefinitely.[40] The U.S.S.R., in opposing the resolution, also believed that lumping several items together would undermine existing standards for sea-bed exploitation.[41]

One reason for hesitation in calling a law-of-the-sea conference is that some governments, including the United States and U.S.S.R., are fearful of a Pandora's box of related issues that might be decided contrary to their wishes. Within governments a struggle is underway to define national interests with respect to the opportunities afforded by advances in marine science and technology. The National Petroleum Council, for example, strongly urges the

United States to stake its claim to resources on the sea bed as far seaward as the continental margin where the submerged land mass meets the deep ocean abyss. Were it adopted, this definition would permit the United States to "acquire permanent exclusive access to the mineral resources of an additional 479,000 square miles of sea bed and subsoil." [42]

The Soviet Union has also appeared recently to doubt the desirability of narrow national limits. It has curtailed American exploration along its northern Siberian coast on the basis of a formula for determining the base lines from which to measure the limits of its territorial waters. Its definition of the territorial sea (twelve miles) would include many straits in its jurisdiction unless specific steps were taken to designate them "international waters." By national edict in 1968, it expanded the definition of the continental shelf to include depressions irrespective of their depth. The littoral powers around the North Sea had previously taken similar action, it is fair to say, to compensate Norway which might otherwise have been at a disadvantage in claiming jurisdiction over petroleum resources owing to the deep ocean trench off its mountainous shores. The Soviet edict goes on to prohibit foreign individuals and companies from carrying out research, exploration, and exploitation of natural resources, and other work on the Soviet Union's continental shelf. Brazil, among other states, also permits such activity only with official permission. The Soviet Union, Poland, and East Germany have signed a declaration that in effect gives Baltic states exclusive rights on the Baltic Sea's continental shelf. In addition, Soviet jurists are reported to be arguing that the seaward boundary of a coastal state on the shelf should not depend upon the technology of that state but rather upon the state of the art, i.e., the exploitive capacity of the most advanced states.[43]

The Regime Beyond National Jurisdiction

The developing countries have pressed hard but so far unsuccessfully for the adoption of another principle important for the U.N.'s future—that the area beyond national jurisdiction should

be considered the "common heritage" of mankind. Ambassador
Pardo urged its acceptance as "the key that will unlock the door
of the future. It is a new legal principle which we wish to introduce into international law. . . ." [44] Sweden also spoke in favor
of the principle, noting that its enforcement would require "some
kind of institutionalized international supervision or regulation of
the use by States of this common heritage." [45]

The linkage of the "common heritage" notion with international or supranational authority in all probability influenced
the Soviet Union to oppose and the United States to abstain when
Resolution 2467C (dealing with international machinery) was put
to a vote. Neither power was prepared to accommodate a majority
of developing countries beyond a less radical statement that the
sea bed should be used for the "benefit of all mankind." Moreover, a draft statement of "agreed principles" by the Western
states in the Ad Hoc Committee made no mention of a "common
heritage" while the developing countries included it as their first
principle in their "agreed" list.[46]

Another issue on which U.N. members divide is the role of
international organizations in regulating the use of the sea bed.
Many developing countries look to the U.N. or some special-
purpose agency to protect their interests in what they consider a
common heritage. The U.S.S.R., on the other hand, has stead-
fastly opposed the establishment of a new ocean body, particularly
if it smacked of supranational authority. The United States also
has warned against the premature establishment of sea-bed institutions. Again, the views of the United States and the U.S.S.R.
are largely congruent.

Venezuela and Kuwait were the first of the developing countries to urge formally that the Sea-Bed Committee "examine the
establishment of international machinery" to regulate the use of
sea-bed resources with particular concern for the needs of developing and landlocked countries.[47] They sought to amend the Belgian
proposal to this effect and gained support from many states, including Sweden. The amendment was opposed by others, however,
particularly the Soviet and Eastern European countries which
noted that common ownership or an international institution to

regulate sea-bed activities directly were unacceptable. Despite the urging of many supporters of the Sea-Bed Committee that this effort be dropped for the time being, Venezuela and Kuwait were joined by Saudi Arabia and Niger as sponsors and were supported by many others also insisting on an immediate study of institutional machinery. Finally, as a concession to the opposition to their amendment among the sixty-six sponsors of the proposal for a Sea-Bed Committee, they abandoned their effort only to revive it as a separate resolution, number 2467C, which carried as noted above.[48] All the Latin American States except Barbados, Jamaica, and Trinidad and Tobago voted for it; as did all the Asian and Middle Eastern States except Jordan, Syria, and Israel; and all the African states except Congo (Brazzaville), Guinea, Madagascar, Malawi, the Sudan, the U.A.R., and Upper Volta. Twelve of the Western States voted in favor, while eleven including the U.S.A., abstained. Yugoslavia voted affirmatively; Cuba abstained; the Soviet bloc voted in the negative.

Opposition lessened the following year when the question of international machinery was discussed again by the General Assembly. A draft resolution, number 2574C, requesting the Secretary-General to prepare a further study of the various types of international machinery, was adopted in the First Committee by 99 votes to 1 against with 13 abstentions. The United States, along with the Latin American states except Cuba, Western European states except Portugal, and Asian and Middle Eastern States voted in the affirmative. The Soviet bloc abstained, with the exception of Mongolia which voted in the negative.[49] The Assembly adopted the resolution by a vote of 100 for to 0 against with 11 abstentions.[50] The United States was in favor, while the U.S.S.R. abstained.

CONCLUSION

How votes will be cast in the future depends on the powers assigned to any institutions planned for a revised international regime beyond national jurisdiction. The Western and Eastern blocs might well be able to agree on a passive agency that would simply register national claims and perhaps provide procedures to settle disputed claims and activities. The United States is seeking such a role for the IOC to promote oceanographic investigation, and there is reason to think the U.S.S.R. will agree. Many developing countries may not be satisfied with a passive type of sea-bed agency, however. Some of them may seek wider authority for an international institution to enable it to issue licenses and supervise sea-bed operations. Senator Pell has introduced a draft treaty to this effect in the U.S. Senate. The Stratton Commission has made essentially the same recommendation. The Center for the Study of Democratic Institutions and the Commission to Study the Organization of Peace have also proposed international institutions having similar authority and functions. However, there is no certainty that the United States will make common cause with such countries.[51] There are strong pressures in the United States to widen national limits and to restrict international agencies. Developing coastal states may also change their views to conclude that their economic and security interests will be protected best by reliance on national authority and by extending national claims. Some of them already feel this is the best way to protect their fishing interests. Some of them seem satisfied with the terms they are able to impose on oil companies from the advanced countries anxious to exploit their offshore petroleum resources. Many are concerned to limit eavesdropping by oceanographic vessels by extending the width of their territorial waters.

Prediction is risky but necessary in international affairs. Accordingly, it seems reasonable to expect that a modest degree of congruence in Soviet and American behavior toward functional cooperation will continue and may even be strengthened by new developments in the oceans and on the sea bed. The United States, to be sure, continues to have more faith than the Soviet Union in the tradition of international organization disinterestedness. Yet each is reluctant to let any agency beyond its control assume important responsibilities over economic resources. More specifically, both have been wary of the General Assembly on sea-bed matters as they are of similar large bodies such as UNCTAD where they tend to be in a permanent minority. They recognize that their capacity to win significant numbers of members to their side by presenting economic questions as East–West issues is conspicuously weak. They are unprepared to meet most of the developing-country demands on North–South issues. The crystal ball seems clear enough to hazard the prediction that the two maritime powers will be anxious to limit U.N. authority and activity on the sea bed and elsewhere. Any significantly expanded role for the United Nations on the sea bed beyond national limits can be expected to fall victim to an uneven but continuing congruence of Soviet and American interests to limit the scope and authority of international organizations.

NOTES

1. U.N. Document A/6695 (August 18, 1967).
2. John G. Stoessinger, *The United Nations and the Superpowers* (New York: Random House, 1965), p. 180.
3. Alvin Z. Rubinstein, "Soviet and American Policies in International Economic Organizations," *International Organization,* Vol. XVIII, No. 1 (Winter 1964), p. 52.
4. Marshall Shulman, "The Soviet Turn to the Sea" in Edmund A. Gullion, ed., *The Uses of the Seas* (Englewood Cliffs: Prentice-Hall, 1968); Edward L. Beach and Stephen B. Luce, "An Appraisal of Soviet Maritime-Naval Capabilities," *Naval War College Review,* Vol. XXI, No. 10 (June 1969), p. 15.
5. Rubinstein, *op. cit.,* pp. 51–52.
6. Rubinstein, *op. cit.,* p. 31; Harold K. Jacobson, *The U.S.S.R. and the U.N.'s Economic and Social Activities* (Notre Dame, Indiana: University of Notre Dame Press, 1963), p. 237.
7. Rubinstein, *op. cit.,* pp. 32–33.
8. Robert S. Walters, *American and Soviet Aid Policies* (to be published by the University of Pittsburgh Press, Fall 1970), Chap. IX, pp. 11–15.
9. Stoessinger, *op. cit.,* Chap. 9.
10. *Our Nation and the Sea, A Plan for National Action,* Report of the Commission on Marine Science, Engineering and Resources, Washington, D.C., USGPO (January 1969), p. 149.
11. Walters, *op. cit.,* Chap. IX, p. 103 and Table II.
12. *Ibid.,* p. 4.

13. J. C. Mills, "Canada at UNCTAD," *The International Journal,* Vol. XX (Spring 1965), p. 214, cited in Harry G. Johnson, *Economic Policies Toward Less Developed Countries* (Washington, D.C.: The Brooking Institution, 1967).
14. Johnson, *op. cit.,* Appendix B, pp. 251–254.
15. Walters, *op. cit.,* Chap. IX, pp. 20–38.
16. Eugene Rostow, "From Aid to Cooperation: Development Strategy in the Next Decade," *Department of State Bulletin,* Vol. LVIII, No. 1498 (March 11, 1968), p. 344.
17. Walters, *op. cit.,* Chapter IX, p. 34.
18. U.N. Document A/6695 (August 18, 1967); *italics added.*
19. U.N. Document A/2340 (XXII) (December 18, 1967); U. N. Document A/2467A (XXIII) (December 1968); italics added.
20. James Simsarian, "Inspection and Experience Under the Antarctic Treaty and the International Atomic Energy Agency," *The American Journal of International Law,* Vol. 60, No. 3 (July 1966), pp. 502–510.
21. Commission to Study the Organization of Peace, "The United Nations and the Bed of the Sea, Nineteenth Report" (New York: Commission to Study the Organization of Peace, March 1969). The CSOP in its Declaration of General Principles recommends that the U.N., in cooperation with its Specialized Agencies and the IAEA, take measures to ensure the observance of the principles.
22. Stoessinger, *op. cit.,* p. 137.
23. *Ibid.,* pp. 139–140.
24. U.N. Document A/AC.135/20 cited on p. 52 of U.N. Document A/7230, *Report of the Ad Hoc Committee;* italics added.
25. U.N. Document A/AC.135/24 in A/7230, p. 54; italics added.
26. Henry Tanner, "U.N. Group Balks on Sea-bed Treaty," *New York Times* (December 13, 1969).
27. U.N. Document A/PV 1752 (December 21, 1968), pp. 13–15.
28. U.N. Documents A/C.1/PV 1602, pp. 48–53; A/C.1/PV 1603, pp. 26–36.
29. This was the Ad Hoc Committee to study the peaceful uses of the Sea Bed and the Ocean Floor Beyond the Limits of National Jurisdiction. It reported to the twenty-third session of the General Assembly (A/7230) prior to the establishment of the Standing Committee.
30. Shulman, *op. cit.,* p. 159; Alexander Dallin, *The Soviet Union at the United Nations* (New York: Frederick A. Praeger, 1962), p. 62.
31. U.N. Document A/PV 1752, p. 16.
32. U.N. Documents A/C.1/PV 1648 (December 19, 1968), pp. 42–43 and A/PV 1752 (December 21, 1968), pp. 16–20.
33. U.N. Document A/PV 1752, pp. 17–20.

34. U.N. Document E/4680 (June 2, 1969), *Mineral Resources of the Sea,* Report of the Secretary-General, p. 15.
35. *Our Nation and the Sea,* p. 145.
36. *Ibid.*
37. *Study on the Question of Establishing in Due Time Appropriate Machinery for the Promotion of the Exploration and Exploitation of the Resources of the Sea Bed and the Ocean Floor Beyond the Limits of National Jurisdiction, and the Use of these Resources in the Interests of Mankind,* Report of the Secretary-General A/AC. 138/12, June 18, 1969, p. 4. The Report on this subject cites the *Report of the Ad Hoc Committee,* Document A/7230, par. 86.
38. Resolution 2574D was adopted in the First Committee by a roll-call vote of 52 in favor to 27 against with 35 abstentions; the Assembly adopted the resolution 62 in favor to 28 against with 28 abstentions. *U. N. Chronicle,* January 1970, pp. 73–74, 76.
39. *U.N. Chronicle,* January 1970, p. 73.
40. Statement of Ambassador Christopher H. Phillips, Deputy U.S. Representative on U.N. Security Council before the Sub-committee on International Organizations and Movements, House Foreign Affairs Committee, March 4, 1970, and Press Release USUN 25 (70) March 4, 1970. See also, Statement of Ambassador Phillips, First Committee, A/C.1/PV 1709, December 2, 1969, pp. 23–25.
41. Mr. Mendelevich, U.S.S.R., Statement before the First Committee, A/C.1/PV 1708, p. 72.
42. This interpretation of the National Petroleum Council's position was given by the Commission on Marine Science, Engineering and Resources, which offers a contrary recommendation, *Our Nation and the Sea,* p. 144.
43. William E. Butler, "Edict 53 on the Continental Shelf, Presidium of the U.S.S.R. Supreme Soviet, February 6, 1968," *American Journal of International Law,* Vol. 63, No. 1 (January 1969), p. 105.
44. U.N. Document A/C.1/PV 1589 (October 29, 1968), p. 27.
45. U.N. Document A/C.1/PV 1596 (November 4, 1968), pp. 28–30.
46. U.N. Document A/7320 (Report of the Ad Hoc Commitee), pp. 17–19.
47. U.N. Document A/C.1/L.426 (October 30, 1968).
48. U.N. Document A/PV 1752, p. 22.
49. A/C.1/PV 1709, pp. 62–63.
50. U.N. Chronicle, January 1970, p. 73.
51. The Pell Treaty was presented as S. Res. 33, 91st Congress, 1st Session, January 1969. See also "The Ocean Regime," Oc-

casional Paper, Center for the Study of Democratic Institutions, Santa Barbara, California, 1969, and "The United Nations and the Sea Bed," 19th Report, Commission to Study the Organization of Peace, New York, March 1969. In this Report, the Commission recommends that the General Assembly establish an International Authority to administer a regime for the orderly exploitation of mineral resources of the sea bed beyond national jurisdiction.

KEEPING THE PEACE: AN INTERPRETATION OF SOVIET AND AMERICAN SECURITY POLICIES *

James Patrick Sewell

In the respective official views of the Soviet Union and the United States, the United Nations organization was created and remains primarily an instrument of national security and, to the extent this is perceived as necessary to national security, of international security as well. Security, a *sine qua non* of national life, informs the vital and marginal interests defined and redefined or reapplied by governments—those individuals who act through the nation-state's major roles. But governments seek security and other values through the United Nations as only one of various alternative means, and in practice the governments of the two superpowers have tended to stress alternative strategic modes and channels rather than the U.N. Security actions through the United Nations have been described by different words and phrases that are deployed with the intention of justifying or condemning specific governmental objectives or international outcomes. These words may aid, nonetheless, in describing and discriminating experiences.

This essay endeavors to interpret Soviet and American initiatives and United Nations outcomes in keeping the peace. Even-

* The author wishes to thank the Office for Advanced Political Studies, Yale University, and Richard Johnson, II, for research assistance on this essay. He is obliged to Alvin Z. Rubinstein and H. Bradford Westerfield for helpful criticism of a previous version.

tually the focus is "peacekeeping," which can be defined inductively as the dispatch of internationally authorized personnel from relatively disinterested third-party states to a holding action, physically or symbolically, between two belligerents who acquiesce in this arrangement and in the cease-fire necessary for its initiation and its continuation. "Preventive diplomacy," in its use by Dag Hammarskjöld, is a comparable notion which shares with peacekeeping the empirically unsubstantiated implication that open hostilities are thereby averted, not merely suspended. Though less exalted, "truce-keeping" more tellingly describes actual cases. Peacekeeping has not forestalled wars; wars have sometimes triggered peacekeeping.

Peacekeeping, a high United Nations official once remarked, lies between Chapters VI and VII of the United Nations Charter. This is, as we shall see, not the only way to characterize the practices here addressed or for that matter to depict their somewhat precarious Charter position, but it does help both to distinguish peacekeeping from and relate it to two other notions. Peaceful settlement, or peacemaking, is the subject of Chapter VI; preventing war and enforcing peace is the declared purpose of Chapter VII.

Peacekeeping outcomes are more modest than those expected from either Chapter VI peacemaking or Chapter VII peace maintenance. Peacekeeping is directed into a situation of conflict in order to freeze it or keep it frozen, quite possibly along lines of a forcibly revised *status quo,* whereas in principle peacemaking would yield a lasting political settlement demanding no continued third-party activity between disputants, and Chapter VII sanctions would either deter entirely or reverse gains resulting from a threat, breach, or act of aggression against the *status quo.*[1]

Like peacemaking, peacekeeping conjures up a vision of third-party mediation between two antagonistic parties. A continuum of U.N.-sanctioned forcefulness might establish peacekeeping (with peacemaking) at one extremity, peace maintenance or enforcement at the other. Actual cases would then range from virtually figurative or token peacekeeping instances such as U.N. "presences" and perfunctory individual investigation of complaints, through observation corpsmen, passively interpositioned forces, and more active policing of temporary agreements or even of volatile situations as such, then on to forcible application of a U.N. judgment upon a duly found aggressor.[2] In the same direction across this continuum the perceived third-party attributes of "U.N." action fade and disappear. The Secretary-General's personal representative as U.N. presence is apt generally to be regarded as disinterested in the best sense of that word; Secretary-General-directed peacekeeping contingents, such as those in the Congo, are more suspect in the eyes of some U.N. participants, if only because their presence as such tips the scales in someone's favor; the Secretary-General-anointed Korean operation was a second-party action supporting one of two belligerents, the putative innocent.[3]

It is no great exaggeration to state that the first quarter century of United Nations security featured actions undertaken by governments outside the U.N.; ex parte enforcement precipitating a façade of collective legitimation; a series of largely unsuccessful attempts at peacemaking; and a few varied peacekeeping operations shaped by the expectations acknowledged above and other constraints surveyed below.

I

No concern among wartime United States policy makers bent on transforming the United Nations from an alliance into a postwar international security organization outweighed the resolve that World War III must not be allowed to happen. This resolve was shared by the American people. Alongside the commitment to peace, however, operated a domestic political premise. After the war, Franklin Roosevelt and various other public figures believed, Americans would not abide continuing international commitments if these demanded stationing their boys across the oceans and shouldering heavy military tax burdens at home. Sometimes efforts to reconcile these policy imperatives produced gimmicks or slogans befitting the domestic political situation as much as security internationally. Growing overseas military commitments, especially from the late nineteen-forties to the present, seem to belie one of the initial premises. Peacekeeping and other security developments must be seen against the background of these stable and shifting assumptions.

Peace on the cheap, or "effortless security" in Eugene Rostow's phrase, was hardly a new political problem for American leadership. Collective security, championed by Woodrow Wilson, offered an alluring formula for international society to avoid war without depriving states of their sovereign autonomy. The surety of collective action by all on behalf of any one victim against any other transgressor would restrain or if necessary repel acts violating the victors' armistice settlement. Before and after such an exceptional mobilization of the multinational fire brigade, or posse comitatus, national life would go on much as always. Collective security was a scheme with apparent gains for everyone and no evident costs for anyone.[4]

During World War II, however, the notion of collective security in effect underwent severe practical modification. Disarmament as a complement to collective security did not receive the attention in United Nations' blueprints for permanent peace that it had had during the League of Nations era. While the public advent of the atomic bomb following the San Francisco conference of 1945 caused some rethinking, the management of force, not the elimination of forcible implements, remained the operative premise—protestations later rising from a politics of disarmament notwithstanding. Force for enforcement in United States planning now assumed a kinetic quality superseding the potential energy implicit during bygone days when a vision of polyglot minutemen, responsive if called but otherwise engrossed in normal peacetime activities, held sway.[5] Most important, this force-in-being was to be managed, singly or jointly, by the powerful leaders of a prevailing grand alliance of United Nations.

The United States would, in wartime prevision and in fact, emerge as the strongest of the victors. Great Britain, her war-precipitated weaknesses momentarily hidden from American and Soviet discernment by lion-hearted Churchillian posturing, was taken as a second pillar of the new framework of international security. Britain was foreseen initially as a stout ally in peace as in war, an ally strong enough to carry sustained responsibility for stability in much of the world, strong enough indeed to allow the

United States and others to share the benefits of intercourse with areas of imperial preference, strong enough—it was recognized from Lend-Lease onward—to resist these American overtures to an "open world." The Soviet Union was apprehended as the third pillar necessary for any lasting peace. Maintaining an Anglo-American alliance with the Soviet Union in order to defeat all the Axis powers and preserve the ensuing settlement constituted a major priority of American and British wartime diplomacy.[6] China was conceived by Roosevelt as a promising check, with American support, against Japanese resurgence; Churchill and Stalin tolerated what they considered a harmless illusion. These powers would become FDR's "Four Policemen." France was later included as a mainstay in United Nations' security designs, partly at the behest of the British.

In official United States expectations, then, the emergent great powers would prevent World War III by enforcing the peace they would establish—and the American contribution to this enforced peace would consist not of American boys stationed indefinitely abroad but of highly mobile, widely based naval and air units capable of deterring or suppressing threats and breaches. Naval power had long enjoyed strong American support, and with World War II developments, including the first primitive nuclear weapons, air power gained new adherents. Vice President Henry Wallace, James Shotwell, and Clark Eichelberger were among pre-Hiroshima advocates of an international air force which could, as Shotwell asserted, reduce international policing to a minimum without risking international anarchy. The 1944 Democratic National Convention platform committee received a similar proposal from Florence Harriman, Claude Pepper, and Carl Hatch—"the good old American principle of collective security," as Mrs. Harriman acclaimed it.[7]

Soviet assumptions about security in the postwar world differed in important respects, although certain early expectations seem remarkably similar to those of U.S. planners. While Americans were inclined to treat peace as a normal condition whose disruption by aberrant war might thenceforth be prevented by inventing the right devices or merely by setting up known mechanisms, Soviet theory regarded struggle at all social levels as the natural state of mankind in each historic phase short of a distant and undefined human destiny. On the other hand, wartime circumstances presented common Axis foes and suggested a dire menace to future Soviet security; no immediate Allied disagreements arose over whose aggressions the United Nations were meant to frustrate. Rather like U.S. planners, although drawing different inferences, the Soviets initially saw Japanese and particularly German threats offset by a preponderant armed concert of the Allied powers.[8]

Gazing backward, no single guiding conception of the postwar world appears to explain the actions either of American or Soviet policy makers. Spokesmen for each system have ascribed to the other one designs for global hegemony. But the insatiable worldly appetite laid respectively by American and Soviet publicists to the iron laws of Leninist Marxism or capitalism surely fall far short as adequate interpretations of foreign security policies during the past twenty-five years. "The American Century," Henry Luce's renowned 1941 *Life* editorial, named a popular sentiment but it offered no more than a poor fit for reserved, even timid U.S. policy immediately following the war. Notwithstanding sporadic Socialist imprecations—and Western inferences—of the burial of capitalism or the spread of earth-covering Communism by other means, Soviet leaders have frequently demonstrated their ability to make pragmatic judgments that recognize a range of variables. As *Pravda* on July 14, 1964, catechized the Chinese People's Republic, "the atomic bomb does not observe the class principle." [9]

Spheres of influence explain more than designs for global hegemony when approaching the evolution of United Nations peacekeeping. No doubt many Americans find distasteful the thought of an extra-national expanse with its peoples over which a great power stands ascendant, whether such a sphere of influence be Soviet or other. But however odious the idea and however tacit or even confused any early Soviet-Anglo-American understandings on its application, a number of subsequent events are illuminated by viewing them as phenomena that occur either within or outside a domain or preserve effectively overseen by the Soviet Union or the United States.

That this notion was not alien to all American founding

fathers of the United Nations security scheme is apparent from contemporary records.[10] "It is planned to make an agreement among the Big Four," wrote Cardinal Spellman after a discussion with Roosevelt on September 3, 1943.

> Accordingly the world will be divided into spheres of influence: China gets the Far East; the US the Pacific; Britain and Russia, Europe and Africa. But as Britain has predominantly colonial interests it might be assumed that Russia will predominate in Europe. Although Chiang Kai-shek will be called in on the great decisions concerning Europe, it is understood that he will have no influence on them. The same thing might become true—although to a lesser degree—for the US. [FDR] hoped, although it might be wishful thinking, that the Russian intervention in Europe would not be too harsh.[11]

Some two years later, following Roosevelt's death, the concern differed but the working concept remained. "I think," said Secretary of War Henry Stimson to his assistant John McCloy, "that it's not asking too much to have our little region over here which never has bothered anybody." Since the Soviet Union was establishing just such a realm in Eastern Europe, it would be in no position to object. Without disagreeing on implications for the Western Hemisphere, McCloy urged more flexibility elsewhere: "We ought to have our cake and eat it too; . . . we ought to be free to operate under this regional arrangement in South America, at the same time intervene promptly in Europe; . . . we oughtn't to give away either asset." [12]

Roosevelt's exchange with Stalin at Teheran over a United Nations framework for postwar security suggests how, at one point in time, the American leader dealt with (or failed to deal with) the tricky relationship between his Four Policemen plan and great-power spheres of influence. Churchill had favored regional councils or committees for Europe, the Far East, and the Americas, a proposal that Stalin also liked. While pressing his own argument for a concert of great powers capable of acting anywhere, if necessary, to crush even a major peacebreaker, FDR was asked if this meant that American troops would be sent overseas. The President immediately balked. Roosevelt admitted that in the event of another threat to Europe and a nonproductive ultimatum to the aggressor, he foresaw only the possibility of U.S. naval and air detachments to support British and Soviet ground forces.[13]

Euphemisms render more palatable or more obscure the facts of global condominium. Around the Soviet Union, earlier "safety zones" have ripened into a "Socialist commonwealth." In the West, "collective self-defense" arrangements (nominally obliged to U.N. Charter Article 51) may disintegrate but "regionalism" and what President Nixon calls "preventive diplomacy" among governments and regimes goes on. Scholars discern a "tight bipolar" international system which loosens as the imperial realms of two lesser great powers, and of other traditional colonialists, break off into nonaligned statehood.

Finally, on the significance for maintaining peace accorded a permanent organization of the United Nations, official spokesmen for the United States and the Soviet Union initially took positions not far apart. For both, from the outset, a United Nations organization was secondary as a means to security.

A United Nations organization was secondary in the sense that its writ would enter into practical effect only after a passage of time. After the postwar *status quo* had jelled, U.S. policy makers foresaw, the United Nations as an organization might become a useful operative agent in maintaining peace.[14] On the face of the matter, similarly, there is no indication that Soviet planners wished an enforcement-fitted U.N. before peacetime lines came into being. Actual difficulties in reaching great-power agreement on peace settlements, with some crucial issues outstanding to this writing, have far exceeded the anticipated time to make the peace necessary for full United Nations peace maintenance. Furthermore, the Charter itself, framed largely by the two superpowers and the United Kingdom, provided in Article 106 for an indefinite transition period "pending the coming into force of such special agreements referred to in Article 43 as in the opinion of the Security Council enable it to begin the exercise of its responsibilities under Article 42," during which time the four Moscow Declaration parties of 1943, with France, would "consult with one another and as occasion requires with other Members of the United Nations with a view to such joint action on behalf of the Organization as may be necessary for the purpose of maintaining international peace and security." [15] A strict interpretation of the Charter might conclude that while U.N. peace maintenance has not yet been tried, almost by definition, its formal preliminaries might now at least be undertaken.

Even when fully established as an instrumentality in keeping the peace, the organization was expected by both Americans and Soviets to remain limited as to the scope of action authorized by the United Nations. Again the Charter discloses formative assumptions through the draftsmanship of the big two plus Britain. Article 33, introducing Chapter VI on peaceful settlement, invites disputants to "seek a solution" first *themselves;* Article 52(2) enjoins Members to try "regional arrangements" before trying the Security Council. It is difficult to escape an inference that by its three founding powers the United Nations organization was meant to serve as a forum of last resort.

The Charter limited potential United Nations action in space as well as time. Article 107, along with Article 53(1), waived United Nations organization control of defeated Germany and Japan, leaving this indefinitely to the unnamed "Governments having responsibility. . . ." Edward Stettinius in 1945 informed the U.S. Senate Committee on Foreign Relations that the task remained "in the hands of the nations which have made victory possible in the present war. They will decide when to transfer this responsibility to the organization." [16] Articles 51 and 52(1) underwrote organizational apparatus, or regional arrangements, embracing spheres of influence into which United Nations action would venture gingerly or not at all.

In no way was Soviet-American mutuality on U.N. limitations more evident than in establishing the Security Council great-power unanimity rule, or "veto."

> The unanimity requirement appeared to many as merely
> a frank admission that no effective collective action could
> be taken by the United Nations without the agreement

of all the great powers. This, of course, was true, as far
as it went. However, to Roosevelt, Churchill, and Stalin
—and, to a lesser extent, even to such men as Stettinius
and Hull—the concept went further than that. They felt
not only that the Organization *could not* act without
great power unanimity but also that the Organization
should not try to act when unity was lacking.[17]

In a similar vein Stalin concluded: "Can one trust that the role
of the United Nations will be sufficiently effective? . . . It will be
effective if the Great Powers that carried on their shoulders the
main burden of war against Hitlerite Germany will act afterward
in a spirit of unity and collaboration. It will not be effective if
this necessary condition is absent." [18] And in his diary Arthur
Vandenberg, Republican U.S. Senator from Michigan, confided
that what struck him about the American position prepared for
Dumbarton Oaks was its conservatism "from a nationalist standpoint. It is based virtually on a four-power alliance. . . . and no
action looking toward the use of force can be taken if any one
of the Big Four dissents. [Cordell] Hull's whole theory is that
there must be continued agreement between the Big Four or the
post-war world will smash anyway. Also, to his credit, he recognizes that the United States will never permit itself to be ordered
into war against its own consent." [19]

In Soviet perspectives, the projected United Nations organization carried forward overtones all too reminiscent of its experience with the League of Nations. Organizational and procedural
features that the Americans and others sought assiduously to
achieve probably struck Stalin and his cohorts (who tended to
identify security with expansion) first as apt bargaining concessions for a freer hand with Poland and perforce with other
Eastern European domains.[20] But with each negotiated turn of
the screw—whether immunity from the veto of certain U.N. questions short of enforcement, invitations to San Francisco and to
charter U.N. membership, or the nature and specific composition
of the secretariat—Soviet leaders grew more suspicious of the new
organization and of their wartime allies' designs for it.[21] At least

one observer sensed an increasing Soviet coolness toward the enterprise between Dumbarton Oaks and San Francisco.[22] Perhaps a dominant wartime emphasis upon survival, with its implications for common if awkward alliance fronts against mortal enemies of Russia, was yielding to a Leninist Marxian view that no effective one-world security organization could operate in a two-world global system. Yet the United Nations would organize in any case; as signatories they—if not the organization itself—might provide marginal insurance against German revanchism; on balance it was safer to be in than out.

If expansion was the Soviet (and indeed the Russian) key to postwar security, kinetic force was in American planning the chief device to guarantee peace. Should it later prove possible to negotiate terms under which nuclear-capable American forces would stand ready to engage in collective enforcement operations with other United Nations' troops, this would of course be a welcome outcome from every standpoint. If not, or at least in the interim, the United States Navy, Air Force, and mobile ground forces would be prepared for action jointly with the British, with others, or if it came to that, alone. Domestic proposals for United Nations enforcement were joined by other proposals for United States enforcement, with or without others' assistance. FDR, sensitive since his unsuccessful Vice Presidential campaign on a 1920 join-the-League plank, to the domestic political difficulties of U.S. participation in entangling international arrangements, himself heeded this thunder on the right as the election of 1944 approached. In his widely read *Problems of Lasting Peace,* for instance, Herbert Hoover (with Hugh Gibson) had in 1942 counseled the separation of enforcement from any postwar international organization.[23] On June 15, 1944, the American President issued an assurance that he was "not thinking of a superstate with its own police forces and other paraphernalia of coercive power," but rather "seeking effective agreement and arrangements through which the nations would maintain, according to their capacities, adequate forces to meet the needs of preventing war. . . ." [24] During the same period Senator Harry Truman scored the Republican platform as "ambiguous" and called upon

his own party to pledge "that the United States will take part
in world affairs this time and maintain the peace by using the
Army and Navy, if necessary." [25]

So persistent has been the American theme of peace through
forcible ex parte (though if possible multilaterally supported)
intervention that it may be well to juxtapose two mildly celebrated proposals by American citizens at points in time approximately equidistant before and after the end of World War II.
Writing in 1924, Miss M. Carey Thomas, organizer and for
twenty-eight years president of Bryn Mawr College, outlined a
"declaration of interdependence" by the United States in order
"to outlaw war." The Thomas plan would "not interfere with the
League of Nations"; nations could, but need not, voluntarily
participate in both or of course in neither. "The chief merit of
the plan," continued Miss Thomas,

> is that it enables the United States, acting, if need be,
> single-handed, to block the will to war. . . . There is
> every reason to believe that Great Britain and her Do-
> minions will join the United States in this Declaration
> of Interdependence as soon as they are invited to do so.
> In which case this mighty combination of the two great-
> est world powers with their joint navies covering the
> globe would be able to outlaw war and enforce peace,
> even without waiting for the co-operation of other great
> nations.[26]

In February 1968, a group of some thirty military, business,
and religious leaders headed by former U.S. Marine Corps General David Shoup and Howard Kurtz, a retired airline pilot,
announced the formation of War Control Planners, Inc. and
indicated their intention to urge President Lyndon Johnson to
create a unit in the Department of Defense to study "global
safety." Mr. Kurtz wanted a "global safety authority" set up by
all nations. Its support would come from "governments, business,
communications fields, foundations, church and civic groups and
the United Nations." [27]

II

The shifting postwar international system, profoundly shaped by the objectives and means of the two superpowers and by the existing character and degree of tension between them, has in turn conditioned governments' strategic choices of the United Nations or alternative channels, their tactics in getting those things they want and avoiding those things they do not want through the United Nations, and outcomes from the interplay of these policies. While most Soviet and American assumptions manifested during the U.N.'s origins remain surprisingly stable throughout this quarter century, subsequent events and developments have contributed to changes in relationships among the organization's members and to certain innovations, notably peace-keeping, in the ubiquitous yet often mutually self-denying national quest for security internationally. Given the incipient organization's tangential relationship to Soviet and American designs for their security in the postwar world, it is hardly illogical that the United Nations has since its founding counted for relatively little in keeping the peace. In mitigating war the U.N. has not, however, been altogether negligible.

The United Nations organization as an available security instrumentality soon received even lower priority in the strategic policies of both superpowers. Soviet control of "buffer" areas to its west and elsewhere, and especially the *de facto* dismemberment of Germany, lessened the officially defined value to the U.S.S.R. of any further great-power security agreements through United Nations auspices. Hence Soviet expansion, in this respect as well as because of its impact upon the United States and other Western Governments, lowered the probability of such agreements. Soviet intentions for Iran, intimated earlier to the Americans, were thereafter rebuffed, in part by exposure in the Security Council. The Greek civil war—initially brought to the same forum by the Soviets, along with the Greek regime, on the former's demand that British troops be withdrawn—was in Western media treated as directed from Moscow.[28] Russia's great-power allies thwarted her claim to Libya and to warm water access, an historic push. While containment of Soviet expansion had already begun, Russian security demands vis-à-vis Germany, reckoned the gravest threat, were in process of fulfillment without necessity of the United Nations.

Britain's weakness from the war, so openly demonstrated by the Labour Government's leadership, softened Anglo-American discord over the future of Britain's imperial estates.[29] Churchill's "iron curtain" speech of 1946, the frantic American assumption of what one participant later called "the job of world leadership . . . with all its burdens and all its glory" by way of U.S. aid to Greece and Turkey, and British determination, in Truman's view, "to wash their hands of the whole matter" of Palestine,[30] were landmarks along the way to hardened lines between two antagonistic global powers. Collective self-defense arrangements such as NATO and the Warsaw Treaty Organization would subsequently confirm the tendency to bipolarity and the growing resort to alternative modes rather than the U.N. for concerting, or legitimizing, security policies.[31]

This was the setting for negotiations on national "armed forces" to stand in readiness for Security Council/Military Staff Committee disposal in case of United Nations "action with respect to threats to the peace, breaches of the peace, and acts of aggression." With success, one or more "special agreements" would have allowed Charter Article 43 implementation to end the security transition envisaged in Article 106. The talks failed. Probably neither the Soviet nor American representatives badly wanted military contingents available to the United Nations, though neither wished the public onus for failure. Mutual suspicions were further aroused by the United States and U.S.S.R. proposals and in turn by their rejection.

Of forty-one proposed articles in a draft agreement stating general principles, twenty-five found agreement among the five permanent Security Council members whose Chiefs of Staff constituted the Military Staff Committee of the United Nations.

Among other things, it was agreed that: (i) the permanent members of the Security Council should contribute initially the major portion of the armed forces; (ii) when carrying out enforcement measures, national forces should be based as directed by the Security Council, and under the Security Council's control, with the Military Staff Committee charged with their strategic direction; (iii) the Security Council might appoint an over-all or "supreme" commander, but contingents would retain their national character, would be commanded by officers appointed by their respective governments, and would be subject to national regulations and discipline. Commanders of national contingents would also have the right to communicate with their own governments on all matters.[32]

Most of the contentious articles pitted the Soviet Union against the other four. Only with regard to over-all force capacity was the United States in a comparable minority position.

1947 PROVISIONAL ESTIMATES [33] FOR OVER-ALL FORCE LEVELS CALLED FOR BY U.N. CHARTER ARTICLE 43

	U.S.	U.S.S.R.	U.K.	France	China
Ground force	20 divisions (later 15)	12	8–12	16	8–12
Air force	3,800 planes (later 2,800)	1,200	1,200	1,275	1,200
Naval force (selected)	3 battleships 6 aircraft carriers	0 0	2 4	3 6	
Assault carrier capacity	6 divisions	0	⅔ div.	1 division	

Force level proposals implied the purposes to which peace maintenance operations might be devoted. Inis Claude observes that "the United States was curiously unwilling to recognize the fact that the terms of reference of the projected international force excluded the possibility of its being used, and therefore the necessity of its being usable, for the purpose of taking enforcement action against major powers. In view of the fact that United States officials had previously recognized and accepted—indeed, insisted upon—this restriction of the organization's capability, it was extraordinary to find a United States spokesman arguing that the Security Council should be equipped to 'bring to bear, against any breach of the peace anywhere in the world, balanced striking forces drawn from the most powerful and best equipped forces that could be provided by the Members,' so that the United Nations could 'enforce peace in all parts of the world.'" [34] In this purpose the British representative, speaking six days later, seemed to concur when he referred to the Article 51 "answer" in the event of a great-power veto. "If any one of the permanent members were to call a halt to the United Nations force," he contended, "the remainder of the United Nations would be entitled . . . to take action against that Member. Their forces, already made available to the Security Council, could legitimately be jointly employed to that end for so long as the Security Council failed to take the measures necessary to maintain international peace and security." [35] These arguments could hardly fail to fan the suspicions of a government already constituting a minority of one.

As to the composition of forces, the Soviet Union insisted upon equal or identical national contingents, while the United States, United Kingdom, France, and China urged comparable forces supplied in accordance with the special military strengths of each participant. The nuclear-capable United States joined by Britain and China and, insofar as this bore upon deterrence of a rejuvenated and vengeful Germany, by France, favored forces poised around the world for swift reprisal; the Soviet Union adamantly opposed this, contending they should remain at home unless called. On bases, too, the split occurred. The Soviets sought a thirty- to ninety-day limit on force deployment beyond the assigned mission unless the Security Council affirmatively extended this assignment. All others held that the decision to withdraw forces should itself be made by affirmative Council decision.

The Soviets, Claude concludes,

feared that an authorization for the stationing of United Nations contingents on foreign bases would provide ideological cover to encircle the Soviet Union. They suspected that the Western powers sought a provision permitting one state to assist others in equipping the contingents assigned to the Security Council in order to gain "an opportunity to influence the policies of these States and thus to occupy a dominant position with regard to the armed forces to be placed at the disposal of the Security Council." Their insistence upon establishing a more rigid rule than the Western powers wished regarding the withdrawal of United Nations forces reflected the suspicion that the West sought to gain "a pretext for the continuous presence of foreign troops in territories of other States." [36]

On the other hand, some Americans suspected that the Soviet plan, if accepted, would (as one observer expressed it) "preclude the possibility of United States forces ever being employed by the Security Council outside the Western Hemisphere." [37]

U.N. Secretary-General Trygve Lie attempted to establish a small emergency "United Nations land force" for violence-ridden Palestine on the limited great-power consensus. Both the American and British Governments, whom he had approached privately, turned him down.[38] Thus ended serious efforts, at least during the U.N.'s first twenty-five years, to create Article 43 agreements conceived variously as the "heart" or the "teeth" of United Nations maintenance of international peace and security.

It was not, however, the end of political contrivance. Unrequited if shy attempts at peacemaking led to continuing U.N. presences in troubled areas beyond the superpowers' spheres of influence, often in decolonizing areas. The Middle East, the Indian subcontinent, and what might be called the Greater Archipelago of Indonesia all contributed to the art of settling for the readily possible. From touring field missions staffed and financed by U.N. member governments—sometimes national representa-

tives already on the scene—these presences gradually came to
include U.N. secretariat personnel and persons answering to the
U.N. Secretary-General whose extended field duty was financially
underwritten at least in part through the United Nations.[39] Well
before 1950 the General Assembly and its Interim Committee
had been utilized to sanction some expeditions and to outline
plans to meet future needs.

Often these initiatives emanated from the secretariat or
from various middle powers. Almost invariably American representatives welcomed and supported them. "Executive capacity"
or, in Dag Hammarskjöld's phrase, the U.N. as "dynamic instrument" was a cherished American aim, especially during the years
of clear-cut U.S. dominance.[40] By now the Soviet veto had become the standard explanation of U.N. impotence to an American public always more prepared than its elected representatives
to bank on this last best hope for peace. It was the United States,
not the Soviet Union, that had remained true to United Nations
ideals. Perhaps indeed it was felt that all the other "senior
wardens of the new peace," to borrow George Fielding Eliot's
earlier phrase, had passed along the job of maintaining world
peace to the United States. An inclination thought to be universal was no doubt mainly American. For Americans the U.N.
was an idealized alter ego, and if "it" had thus far not lived
up to the faith therein invested, "it" had at least not yet turned
against its master. To expand the authority of the Secretary-
General and General Assembly was to strengthen the United
Nations in much the same pragmatic fashion the political system of the United States had developed. From the Government's
shorter-run standpoint, the U.N. was a bully rostrum to impress
upon American constituents its vigilance against Communist
encroachment and a handy dumping-ground for issues domesti-
cally too hot to handle.[41]

For the same objective reasons the institutional inventions
added to conventional U.N. diplomatic auspices were anathema
to Soviet officialdom. Socialist regimes were barred from membership—and the Soviets retaliated by barring others. Much of
the time Lie was merely tolerable, and sometimes he seemed a
pliant tool of capitalist imperialism or, in but a slight variation,

of the Americans. The secretariat appeared to be stacked against the Soviets. Russian nationals were cut out of the internal communications networks on political matters. A "mechanical majority" delivered General Assembly legitimacy, for what that was worth in Soviet eyes, to United States policy, and the Interim Committee threatened to become even more pernicious to defined Soviet interests. Field personnel for U.N. presences were generally drawn from North America and Western Europe, not from the Soviet sphere.[42] Even corporate field presences were highly suspect, for good reason given Soviet premises.

> The period from 1947 to 1950 was the heyday of the United Nations commissions. On almost every important political question, the tendency of the Assembly and the Council was to establish one or more subsidiary bodies, usually with rather vague terms of reference, to deal with the issues on the spot. There were many good reasons for this development, the principal one being that it was difficult and time-consuming to get agreement on meaningful resolutions in either of the two organs. The enthusiastic support the United States gave to this method of operation stemmed largely from its usefulness as a means of restricting the amount of influence the Soviet Union could exercise. Important decisions could be left to those operating in the field, and the members of the Soviet bloc were seldom represented on these subsidiary bodies, while the United States almost invariably played a prominent role. . . .[43]

Yet the Soviets acquiesced in measures they could not stop by voicing strict constructionist views of the Charter. When they felt the appropriateness of the tactic, like others from time immemorial to the present, they walked out.

The Korean episode, so often told, retold, and reinterpreted, was at once a logical extension of these tendencies and a sharp break. Lie banished any doubts that may have remained about his activism—or, in Soviet perspectives, his "neutrality." Some months after the military operation had been mounted, "Uniting for Peace" capped the effort to remodel the General Assembly as a security organ.[44] And a "United Nations" field presence had reached new magnitudes. But substituting massive force for benign observation, itself a departure, set in motion other developments as well.[45]

Most obviously, it reaffirmed with a vengeance to the Soviet Union that there was no safety in dropping out of United Nations participation, even as a gesture. Later, as the approach of the American/United Nations forces toward the Yalu River triggered restiveness by the representative of India and other General Assembly members of the "Menon cabal," the Assembly arena's potential for influencing the governments of politically independent new United Nations members began to enter into Soviet estimates. Two years after Stalin's death, with a package deal leading to sixteen new memberships, the Assembly as a forum attended by Asians and others became even more inviting; with subsequent African admissions its prominence for Soviet purposes would rise even higher. The two-camp thesis yielded to a thesis of two camps plus.

In America, the frustrating experience with limited if seemingly just war, highlighted by the Presidential campaign of 1952 and transition to an elected leader who had vowed to break the stalemate in negotiations, suggested greater circumspection before again rushing Americans to the Asian mainland. The collective self-defense organization—"preventive diplomacy" as it would later be called by the Republican Vice President— was transplanted in Southeast Asia.

III

The golden years of peacekeeping, in the sense of ersatz arrangements that fall within the definition offered early in this essay, were those of Dwight Eisenhower's Presidency and Dag Hammarskjöld's Secretary-Generalship. This period coincided with growing Soviet confidence, sparked by Sputnik and by successful testing of intercontinental ballistic missiles and represented by Nikita Khrushchev's claim of a shift in the correlation of world forces.[46] But the Soviet part in U.N. peacekeeping was essentially reactive, and as catalytic policy makers neither the leader of the other superpower nor the new U.N. Secretary-General initially played a role as important as did Britain and France.

Despite growing symptoms during 1956 of another eruption in the Middle East, the Eisenhower Administration failed to act in ways other than those that hastened the explosion. "I really don't know how much we can do," said Secretary of State Dulles to Emmet John Hughes early in September. "Every day that goes by without some outbreak is a gain, and I just keep trying to buy that day. I don't know anything to do but keep improvising." [47] Perhaps Ike felt hemmed in on both sides by the domestic political situation in an election year. Early in October he reported to Hughes an annoying visit by Senator William Knowland of California:

It's amazing how little some people can understand about the world we live in, even on the simplest level. Look at the Suez—with the British already furious with Dulles and me because we're trying to hold them back. And along comes Knowland to this office yesterday, to sit right down there and say seriously: "Just one thing I ask you to assure me—that you won't let the British drag us into another one of their wars." If that isn't the silliest damn kind of talk! [48]

The Israeli attack mobilized U.S. leadership to hand-wringing and to invocation of the United Nations. A Security Council draft resolution demanding an immediate cease-fire and withdrawal of Israeli troops was rejected by the twin negatives of Britain and France. French and British air strikes hit Egyptian airfields. Again Hughes sets the scene on October 31:

The air at the 7:30 breakfast conference (Adams, Persons, Hagerty, Goodpaster, Hauge, and I) seems thick and heavy with the righteous wrath against Britain that is beginning to suffocate the White House. And the

righteousness even seems petty—as if the *real* crime of
London has been to contrive so thoughtlessly to com-
plicate the President's re-election or at least whittle
down his majority. Indignation finally teeters on the
kind of frivolity that is frightening, as one of the staff,
fatigued and intemperate, blurts out this proposal:
"I've been trying to think of what we should *do*. Well,
perhaps this is the time for a—let's call it a *'Bomb for
Peace.'* It's as simple as this: let's send one of Curt Le-
May's gang over the Middle East, carrying an atomic
bomb. And let's warn *everyone*: we'll drop it—if they
all don't cut this nonsense out." This suggestion was
greeted with the pained silence that was the most polite
reply possible. But the crude fantasy underscored (1)
the capacity of some in this Administration for little
more than parochial, self-preoccupied distress, and (2)
bizarre results attainable from a White House staff
totally untouched by serious experience with foreign
affairs.[49]

As depicted by Arthur Larson, Eisenhower had a U.N.
reflex.

Characteristically, the instant he learned of the attack,
it was to the United Nations that President Eisenhower
turned. . . . His commitment to peaceful settlement
through international agencies as the way to solve international problems was so deep-seated as to be second
nature. When the international agency route was open,
one did not discuss and calculate whether, in all the
circumstances, the objective to be gained might over-
balance the arguments against using violence. The question was not open. . . . There was a new way to handle
international disputes, and Eisenhower methodically re-
sorted to it. . . . Don R. Larson, who was head of the
Political Science Department of the University of Miami,
and a liberal Democrat, once said of Eisenhower: "This

man will above all be remembered in history as the President who said, "Do it through the United Nations."[50]

Hammarskjöld was shocked by the attack. Britain? France? Called to emergency session by the United States among others, the Assembly endorsed a cease-fire and authorized steps by the Secretary-General to secure and supervise it. Lester Pearson of Canada, solicitous of Britain and perhaps of France and Israel, was a prime mover on behalf of an international corps, later christened the United Nations Emergency Force (UNEF). "We have to get them off the hook," he said.[51] Reversing the anticipations of great-power action expressed by U.N. founders, Pearson urged that UNEF be composed of units from middle and smaller states. In these steps U.S. policy makers willingly concurred. Ten states volunteered troops numbering up to 6,000 at one point; these patrolled on Egyptian territory, though not in Israel, until ordered out by Nasser in 1967.

Consequences of the nonevents and events of 1956 are almost imponderable for subsequent Franco-Anglo-American relations, for Soviet influence in the Middle East, and for decolonization. The bitterness already felt toward United Nations "meddling" in British and French affairs was compounded by the experience and by these Governments' tendencies to blame the U.N., rather than the United States or other U.N. members, for "its" blundering intervention.[52] But given the train of events leading through October 1956, the outcome could have been far worse for all hands without interposed U.N. peacekeepers.

Until the muffled American outrage at Franco-British intervention—and beginning again in late November—the United States was by Soviet proclamation the chief villain in these pieces. Noteworthy shifts in Soviet tactics occurred during the same period.

In August and September the United States was castigated as the leader of an attempt to reinstate imperialism through an international administration of the Canal and an Association of Suez Canal Users to pressure Egypt into concessions by threatening a Canal boycott. The Republican administration, it was maintained, wished support from American oil companies in the coming election; the prospect of a Canal boycott would delight them, and if it were actually effected, foreign oil sales financed from borrowed dollars would enslave purchasers.

By mid-October Soviet observers had detected "sharp contradictions . . . between the Western partners" on whether to try "new tactical methods of implementing the old policies." [53] The brazen behavior of the British and French in Egypt—and in the Security Council—called for extraordinary measures: "Since Britain and France have sabotaged the work of the Security Council the responsibility for solving the problem rests with an emergency session of the U.N. *General Assembly*. [Emphasis added.]" "The situation in Egypt requires immediate and vigorous action by the United Nations," wrote Bulganin to Eisenhower; "If such action is not taken, the U.N. will lose its prestige in the eyes of all mankind and will thus collapse." The Soviets suggested that the United States and the U.S.S.R. combine military operations to secure the withdrawal of the British and French. Bulganin upbraided Ben-Gurion for taking retaliation into his own hands rather than using U.N. channels.[54]

Within a few weeks the United States again was first on the Soviet firing line. The United States vote in the Assembly was held to be hypocritical because it did not back specific steps to achieve Anglo-French withdrawal. Egyptians were warned that the Americans intended to use UNEF to aid implementation of U.S. schemes. Later the Americans were accused of just this. Meanwhile the Soviet Union, which had joined so eagerly in Assembly attempts to resolve the immediate crisis, subsequently refused to share the financial burdens of UNEF.

Suez can stand as a bench mark against which to compare peacekeeping continuity and change in the subsequent period. Hammarskjöld quickly set about enunciating a doctrine of filling dangerous vacuums and elaborating a series of multiple-purpose precedents. United Nations peace forces became a favored topic in discussions of the Lebanon, the Congo, Yemen, Cyprus, and the renewal of overt hostilities between India and Pakistan offered opportunities to put some of these ideas to work, though invariably on an *ad hoc* basis underpinned by fragile consent and tentative acquiescence.

In July 1958, despite expressions of caution by his military advisers, Eisenhower acted in response to a plea from Camille Chamoun, President of Lebanon, by swiftly sending American marines to calm a volatile situation with a show of force. The U.N. outcome was not entirely satisfactory from the standpoint of the United States. Arab representatives and secretariat officials reached an accord which, though not exactly what U.S. diplomats had sought, received a U.N. imprimatur. The imminent dispatch of a U.N. observer group to Lebanon allowed the American Government to withdraw its forces with the claim that their job was done.[55]

The Congo case brought out several tendencies that had appeared previously. In other respects it differed notably from the Suez experience.

Like their original responses to the Suez episode, Soviet and American reactions to the Congo incidents of July 1960 moved both Governments toward early endorsement of intervention underwritten by the U.N. Eisenhower turned down a Congolese invitation for U.S. military assistance, urging instead an appeal to the U.N. Both Kasavubu and Lumumba promptly initiated such requests. The Soviets, with the Americans, backed Security Council resolutions in July and August leading to the establishment of the U.N. Operation in the Congo (ONUC), (Opération de Nations Unies au Congo).

But Soviet-American agreement on the uses of United Nations instrumentalities soon proved illusory. Unlike Suez, which temporarily shifted the focus of both Governments to the forcible intervention of others, the Congo vacuum rapidly drew attention to the moves and motives of the rival superpowers. Each originally deemed U.N. action "the least costly way to prevent the other from realizing its objectives,"[56] perceived as the establishment of itself or its system in the heart of Africa. Thus, in the absence of congruent objectives, if not inevitably because of mutual suspicion, only one of the two could regard outcomes with equanimity.

The confused Congo situation contributed to a growing Soviet-American rift over U.N. action. Though UNEF peacekeepers patrolled Middle East cease-fire lines, ONUC peacekeepers found no Congolese peace to be kept. Efforts to make

such a peace, or for that matter simply to fashion a truce, un-
avoidably favored certain Congolese and international participants
over others. Even when Soviet and American aims apparently
converged, as for instance upon the continuation or restoration
of a Katanga integral to the Congo, the complexities of implementation led to new accusations regarding the partiality of the
U.N. Secretary-General and those under his direction.

Political opposition buffeted both American and Soviet policy
makers. Official France and Britain, lobbyists for Belgian and
other financial interests, and U.S. Senator Thomas Dodd, the
"Ambassador to Katanga," among others, bedeviled those in the
Eisenhower and Kennedy administrations who wanted a strong
U.N. stance. Soviet officials sought to heed both the sensitivities
of emerging Africans (themselves of divided counsel) and, from
another quarter, attacks from the Chinese People's Republic. The
Soviet spokesman time and again demonstrated his distress that
a draft United Nations directive failed to excoriate the capitalist-
imperialist aggressors. Soviet anguish reached its most dramatic
moment with a display of Khrushchevian wrath.

Without question United Nations auspices served United
States objectives in the Congo, as officially defined, more than
those of the U.S.S.R.—over the short run. In the words of Jona-
than Bingham, then an American representative at the U.N.,
this operation was "a notable example of a situation where the
policy and actions of the United Nations have been generally in
accord with our thinking, while the Soviet view has been consistently overridden." [57] If certain premises are accepted, the
Congo today likewise suggests that the United States got the
better of the Soviet Union through ONUC and its diplomatic
and logistic context. "In the Congo, in Vietnam, in the Dominican Republic," writes Ithiel de Sola Pool, "it is clear that order
depends on somehow compelling newly mobilized strata to return
to a measure of passivity and defeatism from which they have
recently been aroused by the process of modernization." [58] But
some Americans are wondering whether military regimes such as
that of General Mobutu are the best achievable outcomes of
United Nations or any alternative intervention.

In other respects, too, the returns are incomplete. While

the Soviets failed in their troika *démarche,* they have apparently succeeded in making a successor Secretary-General yet more circumspect about U.N. security measures than he might otherwise have proved. The Congo denouement further served to restrict the General Assembly as a feasible avenue to internationally legitimated intervention, and American postures, approximating the standard Soviet position, seem increasingly to face away from this plenary arena.

Most visibly to Americans, the Congo expedition saddled the United Nations with a large financial deficit. ONUC cost about $10 million per month compared to UNEF's $1.5 million. At mission's end in 1964, ONUC's bill totaled $411 million. The Soviet Union refused to support either "illegal" operation, and U.S. efforts to force the issue, besides failing to change the Soviets' stand, have probably served to make other U.N. members more reluctant to endorse potentially costly peacekeeping without strict procedures which would assure the active consent of all great powers represented in the Security Council.[59] Subsequent peacekeeping operations have reflected this new awareness.

Thus, the Yemen observation mission was authorized by the Security Council and financed by "parties at interest." Both were points Soviet representatives had long pressed. In the field UNYOM achieved a very limited success. At this writing the seven-year Yemeni war appears to be at an end. If so this will have happened because of national reconciliation within a republican framework rather than by virtue of peacekeeping, though UNYOM perhaps helped Egyptian and Saudi Arabian intervenees, like others elsewhere before them, to withdraw with a claim of peaceful accommodation.[60]

Cyprus' troubles aroused Soviet concern that the Mediterranean island was earmarked for service as the base for a NATO multilateral force (MLF) equipped with nuclear weapons. Since this NATO plan has been abandoned, Soviet fears seemingly have subsided. UNFICYP is subject to frequent Security Council reauthorization and to voluntary financial support. Criticized for not joining in this financial support, a Soviet spokesman reportedly responded that the U.S.S.R. contribution consists of allowing the West to utilize the U.N. so as to avoid embarrassment.[61] The "oc-

cupiers," as the Soviets call them, include, along with the peri-
patetic Scandinavians and Canadians, observers from a permanent
Security Council member—Britain. Soviet officials show little
interest in closer involvement, and with the relative isolation
of Cypriot from Greek-Turkish affairs—for the moment, at least
—American officials likewise are less intimately engaged. Quiet
talks have occurred between individual representatives of the
Greek and Turkish communities, and UNFICYP has been reduced somewhat in size, but to date the political situation remains
unsettled and murky.

For a better understanding of Soviet and American policies
and United Nations peacekeeping during this period, several
noncases are also pertinent. Guatemala and Hungary in the fifties
and the Dominican Republic and Czechoslovakia in the sixties
further illuminate the unwritten spheres-of-influence and no-man's
land substratum of contemporary peacekeeping. Each protest of
superpower intervention reached a United Nations forum. The
latter two were adorned by some of the trappings, if not the substance, of collective legitimacy. All four interventions provided
the cold war opposition with some big moments before friendly
media. Yet none occasioned serious resistance by the other superpower. Regarding the Hungarian revolution, for instance, Dulles
transmitted a clear message to the Soviets that the United States
would not intervene.[62] At the U.N., according to one who was
there, "a delegation then headed by Henry Cabot Lodge . . .
was active in the corridors in the phase before the Russian intervention, but active not in support of the Nagy government, but
against it. American aids would insistently tell one that Nagy
was just as bad a Communist as Khrushchev, that the whole dispute was a falling out of thieves, that the Nagy representatives
at the United Nations had an appalling Communist record and
so on. It was only after the Hungarian rising had been definitely
crushed, and no possibility or danger of effective United Nations
and United States intervention remained, that Nagy and his
colleagues came to be hailed as heroes and martyrs by the same
people. . . ."[63]

IV

Two major objectives, one short and one longer in range, have informed authoritative U.S. postures in peacekeeping situations: (*a*) stop Communism; (*b*) establish stable (i.e., Communist-resistant) systems. Other objectives, such as economic benefit (or avoidance of economic loss) and amicable relations with governments who feel strongly about particular controversies, are secondary to the extent they are not subsumed beneath the first and second objectives. Setbacks on economic matters and the disgruntlement of friendly governments may have uncomfortable repercussions, but losses to Communism lead to electoral defeat and retirement to private penitence and public obloquy, if not to the spread of the Red scourge over this and planets yet uncontested.

"The minimum aim of Soviet United Nations policy," writes William Kintner, "is to identify the Soviet Union with the 'wave of the future' and the hopes of underdeveloped countries and to paralyze action in the United Nations unless it furthers Soviet objectives." [64] Obstruction, however, must be weighed against the possibility that the aborted U.N. action would on balance have proved preferable to action mounted beyond Soviet-neutralist surveillance. Beyond survival and security within an expanded realm, the Soviets seek to extend their influence and ways (Russian culture as well as Socialism) through all available means, including United Nations activities that promise net gains. To what extent U.S.S.R. influence and ways are intended to exclude those of all others remains an open though tantalizing question.

Whether the Soviet Union or the United States has benefited more from United Nations peacekeeping operations and their side effects, on the assumption that both do not gain equally, must remain a question partly unanswered. Two summary evaluations can serve as boundary judgments for any such assessment. According to William Kintner, "American power has often been neutralized in United Nations disputes, whereas Soviet power has been rendered effective beyond its normal reach." Conor Cruise O'Brien, to the contrary, maintains that the "major decisions of the United Nations on Iran, on Palestine, on Korea, on keeping China out of the United Nations and keeping Formosa [sic] in China's Security Council seat, on Suez, on Hungary and on the Congo have one thing in common: they were all in line with United States . . . policy. . . ." [65] Immediate outcomes, at least, have thus far generally favored U.S. preferences. The absence of global conflagration benefits both leading protagonists, though the exact contribution of peacekeeping firebreaks to this status is disputable. Future peacekeeping proposals are likely to appear palpably beneficial to both American and Soviet leadership—the latter bearing a higher threshold of skepticism—or else fail to achieve U.N. sanction beyond that accorded the volunteer peacekeepers and facultative finance characterizing recent instances.

The impact of Soviet and American policies upon development of United Nations peacekeeping may be somewhat more easily judged, if it is analytically possible at all to separate "the U.N." from its two key components.

Political hostility between the superpowers has meant failure to date on the original, and still the soundest, Charter foundation for a broad range of security measures in keeping the peace. However, the use of lesser power field personnel, an achievement due more to the qualified forbearance than the policies of these two, is an innovation to be reckoned with if ever it is fitted to the political support implicit in piecemeal Soviet-American détente. With troubles along the Soviet and American peripheries of the global condominium, problems at home, a common recognition of the danger of accidental war, and premonitions of a Chinese People's Republic increasingly active upon the stages of the world, the international temperature may be right to forge understandings that will permit future peacekeeping engagements to be joined to negotiated political settlements instead of mutual recriminations and United Nations bankruptcy.

Past peacekeeping missions have been dispatched in lieu of genuine *rapprochement* among antagonists. Future missions may depend upon concurrent if embryonic political settlement. In the Middle East, for instance, blue berets are unlikely to find acceptance unless Israel relinquishes territory it occupied in 1967, and this, in turn, is unlikely to occur unless Arab governments extend to representatives of the Israeli people the recognition of that right to survive that is implicit in face-to-face negotiations. The welfare of Palestinians likewise demands recognition. Given such auspicious circumstances, peacekeeping interposition would become more plausible though less important. Without such circumstances, even peacekeeping along recognized boundaries seems impossible. Thus, the Israeli Government in April 1970 evidently refused to countenance U.S. emissary Joseph Sisco's proposal of United Nations observers on the Lebanese border.[66] Besides the subsequent human tragedies this might have obviated on both sides of the line, U.N. peacekeepers would perhaps have strengthened the hand of the Lebanese Government vis-à-vis resident guerrilla forces and provided an analogue for further efforts in the Middle East.

If political composition with or without peacekeeping is to obtain, here as elsewhere Soviet-American symmetry in restraining local allies and in reminding them of their abiding interests is imperative.[67] Given sufficient concord on details and timing, the Security Council resolution of November 22, 1967, establishes an ample framework for lasting settlement, including demilitarized zones to guarantee "the territorial inviolability and political independence of every State in the area" and a Special Representative—Gunnar Jarring during the years following 1967—to facilitate mutual accommodation.

Is there a future for U.N. peacekeeping in Southeast Asia? Short of containing Chinese influence, there would seem to be little Soviet incentive for a U.N. mission, though one might be tolerated under the formula of silent acquiescence and financial nonparticipation. If it is true, as Bernard Gwertzman divines, that a central Soviet aim is "the isolation of the United States and the gradual erosion of its influence on the world scene," [68] continued American involvement in Indochina probably furthers this aim. Should the Nixon administration decide to initiate in this area the "spheres of restraint" recently commended by Under Secretary of State Elliot Richardson—thereby terminating what the President has called the American role of "peacekeeper in the Asian world"—it might find, difficulties due to U.N. nonmembers notwithstanding, that United Nations peacekeeping can facilitate orderly extrication by absorbing some of the political liability for a redeployment of American forces. Here too the lasting way is also the more difficult: serious negotiations by all interested parties leading to a political settlement.

NOTES

1. For more on these and other international organization assignments, see my "Policy Processes and International Organisation Tasks," in Robert W. Cox, ed., *International Organisations: World Politics* (London: Macmillan, 1969).
2. Cf. David P. Forsythe, "United Nations Intervention in Conflict Situations Revisited: A Framework for Analysis," *International Organization*, 23 (Winter 1969), pp. 132–33, to which this scale owes several of its points. Other provocative categories are utilized by Alan James in *The Politics of Peace-Keeping* (New York: Praeger, 1969).
3. For observations that fuzz the U.N. finding on responsibility for the Korean outbreak, see I. F. Stone, *The Hidden History of the Korean War* (New York: *Monthly Review*, 1952).
4. An incisive critic of collective security is Inis L. Claude, Jr. See especially his *Power and International Relations* (New York: Random House, 1962) and *Swords Into Plowshares,* rev. ed. (New York: Random House, 1964). For a varied collection of comments, see Marina S. and Lawrence S. Finkelstein, comps. and eds., *Collective Security* (San Francisco: Chandler, 1968).
5. Here are two recent examples of kinetic-force thinking: "When we get the really big planes, we shall see in other parts of the world as well the positioning of forward equipment, with more of our forces maintained in the center but capable of quick movement. That will have to evolve with the big aircraft." "Q[uestion]. Are you looking forward to an era [when] you could cope with problems in the Middle East, Far East, Africa, and so forth, on that kind of basis?" "A[nswer]. Yes. Remember, you must have first a deep political understanding with the countries [sic] concerned that they want to have this kind of security relationship. Second, you must have overseas bases which are secure which contain some of the heavy equipment. We are now talking about things that are for the seventies, we are talking of a future trend, not a policy as a fact. But I believe that is the way our military posture will gradually change." Walt W. Rostow, interview with *The New York Times,* reported January 5, 1969,

p. 14. "I want to say here and now that people who really mean
it when they say we should bring these troops home [from Viet-
nam], had better provide for the airlift because you are not going
to be able to bring them home until you have some means to
send them back." Senator Stuart Symington, quoted in *I. F.
Stone's Weekly*, September 22, 1969, p. 2.
6. Lawrence D. Weiler and Anne Patricia Simons, *The United
States and the United Nations: The Search for International
Peace and Security* (New York: Manhattan, 1967), Chap. 1. Thus,
at Dumbarton Oaks in 1944, the U.S. Joint Chiefs of Staff urged
that the procedural impasse on voting not be allowed "to endanger our relations with the Soviet Union." Quoted from *The
Memoirs of Cordell Hull* by Weiler and Simons, *op. cit.*, n. 9,
p. 5.
7. Robert A. Divine, *Second Chance* (New York, Athenaeum, 1967),
pp. 80ff., 173, 185, 212. Norman Thomas derided such schemes
for "Peace through the Police."
8. Cf. Weiler and Simons, *op. cit.*, p. 47.
9. Quoted in William Zimmerman, *Soviet Perspectives on International Relations, 1956–1967* (Princeton: Princeton University,
1969), p. 5.
10. To some, including Secretary of State Cordell Hull, it was familiar but repulsive.
11. Quoted in Hans J. Morgenthau, "Historical Justice and the Cold
War," a review of Gabriel Kolko, *The Politics of War*, New York
Review, July 10, 1969, p. 15.
12. Quoted in *ibid.*, p. 16.
13. Robert Sherwood, *Roosevelt and Hopkins*, II (New York: Ban-
tam, 1950), pp. 411–412.
14. Cf. Divine, *Roosevelt and World War II* (Baltimore: Johns
Hopkins, 1969), pp. 57, 58, 61.
15. "The smaller states can be coerced. Therefore, a problem of
primary importance in the development of security organization
is the establishment of a satisfactory relationship between the
large-state suppliers, and the small-state consumers, of security.
For the first period after the war, it may be asumed that such
security measures as are determined upon will be on an *ad hoc*
basis in which there will be no formal arrangements for consultation with the smaller powers affected. The real problem arises
in connection with the second period in which a permanent organization will exist. In shaping this organization it will be
necessary to work out arrangements which will give the smaller
powers a voice in the determination of security policy, but which
will leave the final decision in the hands of the great powers

who will have the responsibility for its enforcement." Grayson L. Kirk, "International Politics and International Policing," Memorandum No. 9, Yale Institute of International Studies, March 10, 1944, p. 9; see also pp. 11–12. See, further, Kirk and Percy E. Corbett, "The Outlook for a Security Organization," Memorandum No. 10, same series, June 15, 1944, pp. 8–9; Weiler and Simons, *op. cit.*, pp. 41–42, 49–52. Reporting to the President, Edward Stettinius added two conditions to termination of the transition period, "the state of world affairs" and "the rapidity with which the new Organization demonstrates its capacities." Quoted in Weiler and Simons, *ibid.*, pp. 50–51.

16. Quoted in *ibid.*, p. 50; see also pp. 79–80.
17. *Ibid.*, p. 40. Cf. Claude, "The United Nations and the Use of Force," *International Conciliation*, 532 (March 1961), pp. 329f.
18. Quoted, from S. B. Krylov, *The History of the Founding of the United Nations* (Moscow, 1960), by Adam B. Ulam, *Expansion and Coexistence* (New York: Praeger, 1968), p. 412. Ulam's interpretation is equally cogent: "The basic Soviet attitude [at Dumbarton Oaks] was entirely realistic, unsinister, and aboveboard. If the Big Three could work together, then peace could be preserved. If not, no formulas, organizations, etc., could guarantee it." P. 372.
19. Quoted in Weiler and Simons, *op. cit.*, p. 32.
20. Ulam, *op. cit.*, pp. 372ff.
21. Cf. Wojciech Morawiecki, "Institutional and Political Conditions of Participation of Socialist States in International Organizations: A Polish View," *International Organization*, 22 (Spring 1968); Alvin Z. Rubinstein, *The Soviets in International Organizations* (Princeton: Princeton University, 1964), pp. 346–348; Alexander Dallin, *The Soviet Union at the United Nations* (New York: Praeger, 1962), p. 127.
22. Franz B. Gross, "The United States National Interest and the United Nations," in Gross, ed., *The United States and the United Nations* (Norman: Oklahoma University, 1964), p. 30.
23. Reported in Divine, *Second Chance*, pp. 60–61. See p. 78 on the continuation of this Hoover theme.
24. Quoted in Claude, *Swords Into Plowshares*, p. 63.
25. Quoted in Divine, *Second Chance*, p. 212.
26. In *Ways to Peace*, a compilation of individuals' plans introduced by Esther Everett Lape (New York: Scribner's, 1924), pp. 169–170.
27. "Group Gives Plan for World Peace," *New York Times*, February 19, 1968, p. 14. U.S. Commander-in-Chief Lyndon Johnson once vowed on behalf of United States efforts in Vietnam that "we must seek out the enemy and deter him." On this theme and "unilateral preference," see my "United Nations and Peacemak-

ing," *Ventures,* 8 (Spring 1968), also H. Bradford Westerfield, "When to Intervene with Force in Politics Abroad? A Pattern in U.S. Decisions," *Ventures,* 8 (Fall 1968). For a more hopeful appraisal of American education in multilateralism, cf. "RFD," "Unilateral and Multilateral Options in the Execution of Foreign Policy," *International Organization,* 23 (Summer 1969).

28. "Impressive silence reigned in Russia while hordes of Greek Communists were mowed down by British and royalist bullets. Stroking his pepper-and-salt mustache in Yalta, two months later, Stalin had a twinkle in his eye for Churchill, as if to say: 'You handled your Greek mess all right.'" John Lukacs, "The Night Stalin and Churchill Divided Europe," *New York Times Magazine,* October 5, 1969, pp. 40, 42. Already its leading actors had discovered the possibilities of the United Nations for staging morality plays. Cf. Conor Cruise O'Brien and Feliks Topolski, *The United Nations: Sacred Drama* (New York: Simon & Schuster, 1968).

29. On the importance of this breach for the specialized agencies, see my essay in Richard Falk and Cyril E. Black, eds., *The Future of the International Legal Order,* IV (Princeton: Princeton University, forthcoming).

30. Joseph M. Jones, *The Fifteen Weeks* (New York: Viking, 1955), p. 7; Harry S. Truman, *Memoirs,* II (New York: Doubleday, 1956), p. 157.

31. "The North Atlantic Treaty was one more step in the evolution of our foreign policy, along with the United Nations Charter, the Greek-Turkish Aid Program, and the Marshall Plan." Truman, *ibid.,* p. 240.

32. Weiler and Simons, *op. cit.,* pp. 131–132.

33. Data from Weiler and Simons, *op. cit.,* p. 135. Further details in *Yearbook of the United Nations, 1947–1948* (U.N.: Department of Public Information, 1949), p. 495.

34. Claude, "The United Nations and the Use of Force," *op. cit.,* pp. 349–350, quoting from *SCOR,* 2nd Year, 138th Mtg., June 4, 1947.

35. Quoted in Ruth B. Russell, *The United Nations and United States Security Policy* (Washington: Brookings, 1968), p. 121.

36. Claude, "United Nations and Use of Force," *op. cit.,* p. 353, and documentary sources cited.

37. Joseph E. Johnson, "The Soviet Union, the United States, and International Security," *International Organization,* 3 (February 1949), as quoted in Weiler and Simons, *op. cit.,* p. 132.

38. Russell, *op. cit.,* p. 122; Trygve Lie, *In the Cause of Peace* (New York: Macmillan, 1954), pp. 166, 187, 192f.

39. See further Russell, *op. cit.,* pp. 161ff., and sources cited; Evan

Luard, "United Nations Peace Forces," in Luard, ed., *The Evolution of International Organizations* (New York: Praeger, 1966).

40. Cf. Cruise O'Brien's thumb rules of delegates in "Conflicting Concepts of the U.N.," his Montague Burton Lecture at Leeds University.

41. As Truman recalled reactions to U.S. (and his own) policy on Palestine, a policy that paused short of support for any U.N. implementation of a political settlement: "Many Jews . . . chose to believe that our Palestine policy was the same as the Zionist program for the State of Israel. Whenever it failed to conform, they would charge that we had turned pro-Arab. The Arabs, of course, looked at our attitude in an even more partisan and hostile light. The simple fact is that our policy was an American policy rather than an Arab or Jewish policy. . . . But the issue was embroiled in politics, not only with us but abroad too. The Jews were for partition—but not all the Jews. The Arabs were against partition—but could not agree how completely they were against it. . . . It was a discouraging prospect indeed. . . . But the matter had been placed in the hands of the United Nations, and, true to my conviction that the United Nations had to be made to work, I had confidence that a solution would be found there." *Memoirs,* II, p. 157. On divergent forces in American domestic politics, see pp. 153–154, 158–159, 160, 167–168. A more recent account is Robert H. Phelps, "Mideast Lobbies: Uneven Match," *New York Times,* April 6, 1970, p. 1.

42. The U.S.S.R. representative accused Swedish Palestine mediator Folke Bernadotte of subordinating himself to United States and United Kingdom objectives in the Middle East—a neat trick, by Soviet standards, given the struggle between these two irreconcilable capitalist systems in the area. While Truman justified his actions toward Jewish refugees and toward Israel as an effort to redeem the Balfour Declaration, and Bevin wrote it off as a stratagem to preempt Thomas Dewey's suit of American Jewish votes, the Soviet tried to explain United States zigs and zags by American intentions to supersede British and French oil interests and by the "enslaving agreement" granting an Israeli market for United States petroleum (a contract later matched for a time by a similar Soviet-Israeli agreement).

43. Weiler and Simons, *op. cit.,* p. 223.

44. Perhaps it is more than coincidence that Dulles, an adviser to Republican Presidential candidates, had just declared that Charter Article 10, on the General Assembly, had been installed at the outset to allow future recommended action in the event a great power exercised its Security Council veto.

45. A contemporary report on Soviet concern was provided by Dean Rusk of the Department of State to C. L. Sulzberger and re-counted in the latter's *Long Row of Candles* (pp. 579, 581 here): "The Russians have made it clear in recent conversations that they are particularly worried about what they call 'the assumption of world leadership' by the United States. They point out that America has military missions in many countries bordering the Soviet Union, such as Turkey and Iran; that we have military bases in areas much closer to the U.S.S.R. than they are to the United States. Although we constantly assure them that we have no aggressive intentions, frequently important American officials make jingoistic statements. They understand what we say to them officially, but they really wonder if this is not a trick game, and if the jingoistic statements, in reality, do not represent actual American policy. . . . By readjusting the balance of responsibility in Korea, we can more easily convince the Russians and Chinese that we don't want bases there."

46. Lincoln P. Bloomfield, *The United Nations and U.S. Foreign Policy* (Boston: Little Brown, 1967 edition), pp. 69–70; Zimmerman, especially chapters 4, 5, and Soviet sources cited.

47. Hughes, *Ordeal of Power* (New York: Athenaeum, 1963), pp. 177–178. See also the *New York Herald Tribune* editorial ("Too Little and Too Late") excerpted by Hughes at p. 210. For thoughts on what might have been undertaken through United Nations auspices, see Bloomfield, *op. cit.,* pp. 168–169.

48. Hughes, *op. cit.,* p. 193.

49. *Ibid.,* p. 218.

50. Larson, *Eisenhower: The President Nobody Knew* (New York: Scribner's, 1968), pp. 55, 56, 67. Arthur Larson contrasts this habit of the administration he served with the inclinations of the two administrations that followed. See pp. 85ff., 120–122.

51. Andrew Boyd, *United Nations: Piety, Myth and Truth* (Baltimore: Penguin, 1964 edition), pp. 105–106.

52. Cruise O'Brien, Montague Burton Lecture *op. cit.,* is especially shrewd on this use of the U.N. as a "lightning conductor" to take the charge off one's own foibles or misdemeanors. The metaphor is attributed also to a former U.S. ambassador to the Congo by Ernest W. Lefever in *Uncertain Mandate* (Baltimore: Johns Hopkins, 1967), p. 77.

53. G. Ratiani, "New Threats Against Egypt," *Pravda*, October 18, 1956; *Current Digest of the Soviet Press (CDSP)*, Vol. 8, No. 42, p. 15.

54. "Message from the Chairman of the U.S.S.R. Council of Ministers, N. A. Bulganin, to President of the United States . . . ,"

162 SOVIET AND AMERICAN POLICIES IN THE UNITED NATIONS

in *Pravda, Izvestia,* November 6, 1956; *CDSP,* Vol. 8, No. 45, p. 23; Bulganin exchange with Ben-Gurion is in *CDSP,* Vol. 8, No. 46, pp. 24–25.

55. Cruise O'Brien, Montague Burton Lecture, *op. cit.*

56. Ernest W. Lefever, "The Limits of U.N. Intervention in the Third World," *Review of Politics,* 30 (January 1968), reprint p. 4.

57. "One Nation, One Vote—and One U.N.," *New York Times Magazine,* September 16, 1962, p. 86; quoted by Claude, *Swords Into Plowshares,* op. cit., p. 300.

58. "The Public and the Polity," in Pool, ed., *Contemporary Political Science* (New York: McGraw-Hill, 1967), p. 26; quoted by Sheldon S. Wolin, "Political Theory as a Vocation," *American Political Science Review,* 63 (December 1969), p. 1065. Cf. Lefever, *Uncertain Mandate, op. cit.,* p. 93.

59. The pragmatic Soviet approach to the future is succinctly stated in an excerpt from U.N. document A/AC.113/39 of September 25, 1965: "[T]he question was raised as to what should be done about financing the future operations of United Nations armed forces. On the face of it, this question is completely abstract and rhetorical. Obviously it is quite impossible to evolve a formula suitable for all future cases in which United Nations armed forces may be employed, a formula which could be uniformly and indiscriminately applied to all operations that might be undertaken in the future. . . . In one case, possibly, the State concerned may forego any claim to payment in respect of the forces it has furnished; in other cases it may be that other decisions will be taken. But it must be said that, for the future, all this will depend on specific circumstances, which at present are completely in the air and impossible to foresee."

60. Dana Adams Schmidt, "Three Mideast Issues Seem Near Solution," *New York Times,* April 8, 1970, p. 10.

61. Alan James, *op. cit.,* p. 437.

62. Speech to Dallas Council on World Affairs, October 27, 1956, cited by Bloomfield, in Bloomfield, *et al., International Military Forces* (Boston: Little Brown, 1964), pp. 30–31.

63. Cruise O'Brien, Montague Burton Lecture, *op. cit.* With suitable substitutions of phraseology, including "Brezhnev Doctrine" for "Monroe Doctrine" where appropriate, the following policy guideline offered in 1904 by Theodore Roosevelt might almost apply to the two more recent superpower interventions: "All that this country desires is to see the neighboring countries stable, orderly and prosperous. Any nation whose people conduct themselves well can count upon our hearty friendship. If a nation

shows that it knows how to act with reasonable efficiency and decency in social and political matters, if it keeps order and pays its obligations, it need fear no interference from the United States. Chronic wrongdoing, or an impotence which results in a general lessening of the ties of civilized society, may in America, as elsewhere, ultimately require intervention by some civilized nation, and in the Western Hemisphere the adherence of the United States to the Monroe Doctrine may force the United States, however reluctantly, in flagrant cases of such wrongdoing or impotence, to the exercise of an international police power." Quoted by Gross, *op. cit.,* p. 25.

64. "The United Nations Record of Handling Major Disputes," in Gross, ed., *op. cit.,* p. 122.
65. Kintner, in Gross, *ibid.,* p. 121; Cruise O'Brien, Montague Burton Lecture, *op. cit.* To this judgment the latter adds, writing elsewhere, that only in America "does the illusion persist that the U.N. is an organization run by Africans for the purpose of thwarting and tormenting Uncle Sam."
66. James Feron, "Israel Said to Bar U.N. Unit," *New York Times,* April 18, 1970, p. 7.
67. Leonid Brezhnev's remonstrance to one disputant is all too relevant to others in this ominous situation: "There is a saying that a wise man learns from the mistakes of others. . . . By its aggressive policy the shortsighted Government of Israel places in jeopardy the security of its own people, whose future lies in good-neighborliness and not in antagonism to the Arabs." *New York Times,* April 15, 1970, p. 17.
68. "Moscow's Goal: Isolation of U.S.," *New York Times,* May 13, 1970, p. 2. or more on U.N. possibilities and limitations in Southeast Asia, see Lincoln P. Bloomfield, *The U.N. and Vietnam* (New York: Carnegie Endowment for International Peace, 1968), and Cruise O'Brien, "How the U.N. Could End the War," New York *Review,* March 28, 1968, pp. 22ff.

THE RULE OF LAW AND THE PEACEFUL SETTLEMENT OF DISPUTES *

Edward McWhinney

To introduce the term "Rule of Law" into a comparative analysis of Soviet and American strategies and practice in the United Nations is to run the risk of prejudging the issue from the start. The "Rule of Law" had a reasonably precise meaning in those late-nineteenth-century English constitutional law teachings in which it had its origins. It connoted a certain procedural, adjectival law-based approach to constitutionalism, with a certain substantive law philosophy inherent in that institutionally oriented approach. Translated to contemporary, post-World War II North America, where it has become a favorite catchword of groups like the American Bar Association, the World Federalists, and perhaps even the American Branch of the United Nations Association, the Rule of Law, in its popular manifestations at least, has seemed too often to be no more than a convenient synonym —a respectably vague formula, if you wish—for rendering in legal form whatever American self-interest may happen to dictate as the national policy in a particular situation. We will do better if we abandon the term "Rule of Law" in its substantive aspects— and, for that matter, the corresponding Soviet formulation, the "Principle of Socialist Legality"—in favor of a conception that

* Some of the points in the ensuing discussions are developed in greater detail in the author's recent studies, *"Peaceful Coexistence" and Soviet-Western International Law* (1964); *International Law and World Revolution* (1967); *Conflit idéologique et Ordre public mondial* (1970).

is more genuinely objective and more nearly neutral with respect to values.

In this essay we are looking for those parts of the Soviet and the American *Weltanschauungen* that involve distinctive national attitudes toward the concepts of world government and of a single, universal system of world law in general; and toward the role of law—here international law—in the resolution of international conflicts and in the promotion of societal change in the present-day world community.

In trying to answer these questions we shall bear in mind the prime lesson of the Continental European, and lately of the North American, sociological schools of law, namely, the basic distinction between the law-in-books and the law-in-action— between what authoritative national decision makers say they are doing and what they actually do in practice. Empirical study of the concrete records of Soviet and American national practice in the arena of the United Nations reveals that the distinction between what Harold Lasswell calls the legal "folklore" (the a priori, high-level philosophical formulations) and (in Ehrlich's phrase) the actual "living law" (the *de facto* attitudes and practices of governmental decision makers) may be quite as significant in the case of the United States as in the case of the Soviet Union. In any case, neither country has an unbroken record of monolithic solidarity or consistency since the end of World War II, but rather an occasionally fluctuating series of responses to rapidly changing power-political situations in the United Nations and in other specialized institutional arenas of Soviet-United States confrontation.

Nevertheless, over the long haul since 1945, a sufficient consistency of national attitudes, expectations, and approaches, has emerged for us to identify fairly easily a "Russian position" and an "American position" on international law and international organization generally; and also the particular political and social facts in the post-1945 world community to which those respective national positions represent a response.

The main dilemma for Soviet international lawyers has always been in the realm of legal theory. Since law, in Marxist terms, is a product of the market place and each economic system thus gets the body of law appropriate to its stage of economic development, how may two different economic systems—capitalism and communism—yield identical bodies of international law doctrine? Or, putting it in more traditional Marxist language, if international law, like national law, belongs to the superstructure and is determined uniquely by the base of productive relationships, how can radically different bases yield the same superstructure of international law?

Pashukanis, perhaps the greatest of the Soviet legal theorists, had tried to resolve the dilemma in the mid-1930's by his celebrated distinction between *form* and *content:* though the *forms* of international law might be identical for all states, opposing social systems could avail themselves of these for their own particular social ends. The long-lived and eloquent Professor Korovin had flirted at times with legal nihilism and the denial of any general body of international law common to both main competing political-ideological systems of the world. He had also considered the theoretical possiblity that universally recognized principles and norms of international law, such as they might be, could be "identical norms of various legal superstructures." In his latter-day writings, in the years immediately preceding his death, Korovin became increasingly seduced by Manichaean notions involving the idea of a good and a bad international law—the only good or true being a more universal, allembracing, "socialist" international law reflecting variously the "collapse of imperialism; the abolition of the colonial system; the transition on to the socialist road of more and more people and the victory of socialism on a world scale."

Korovin's generally reserved or nihilistic attitudes toward the possibility of the existence of general international law rules common to and binding upon all social systems were severely condemned by Soviet official spokesmen and especially by Professor Gregory Tunkin, at the time the Principal Legal Adviser to the Soviet Foreign Ministry and Premier Khrushchev's main technical legal spokesman. Professor Tunkin saw Korovin's "heresies" as to the impossibility of the existence of any general international law as leading objectively to a justification of the "position of strength" policy and of the cold war. As Professor Tunkin commented at the time:

> Difference of ideologies has always existed. . . . For thousands of years jurists have not been able to agree on what is law. And still throughout all this time law existed. So states may profoundly disagree as to the nature of norms of international law, but this disagreement does not create an insurmountable obstacle to reaching an agreement relating to accepting specific rules as norms of international law.

As attractively and persuasively formulated by Professor Tunkin, especially in his elaborations under the rubric of the International Law of Peaceful Coexistence, Soviet international law seems to have moved rather close to the Western pragmatist-realist test of asking only whether international relations exist *de facto* between opposing social systems, and if so, what are their legal manifestations and legal machinery, without inquiring as to their theoretical basis or justification. In the sense in which the great German legal theorist Jellinek postulated it, the factual thus in time gives way to or becomes the normative.

Nevertheless, if the official Soviet governmental position expressed in modern times has been to recognize affirmatively the existence of general international law rules binding on all social systems, it is also true, as a concomitant, that the long-range Soviet position has been characterized by insistence on the untenability of any concept of a world state, and of a world law derived from it—meaning here a legally paramount international governmental or political-institutional authority, and a single, overarching body of universally valid legal propositions and norms deduced logically from such an authority. In the Soviet view, the quest for "Mondialism"—as Soviet jurists derisively label it—runs counter to the elemental facts of life of the contemporary world community where we have no homogeneous political society (as is so often the case with viable systems of internal, municipal or national law). We have rather a plurality of political, cultural, and economic systems dominated, of course, by the twin, competing, ideological blocs and their respective bloc leaders, the Soviet Union and the United States. To insist on a world state or world government as a national policy objective under immediate societal conditions in the world community is, in the view of Soviet jurists, at best to be thoroughly unempirical; at worst, to be simply using the semantic confusion of a seemingly universal aspiration as a convenient cloak for naked power ploys. The Soviet response to its own denial of the possibility of "Mondialism," on any realistic basis under present societal conditions in the world community, is not a descent, at the theoretical level at least, into mere legal nihilism. It is in many respects quite a sophisticated, philosophically pluralistic approach that has some elements in common with contemporary Western concepts of pluralistic federalism in municipal or national law. It is an approach that insists on proceeding from the factual or existential situation in the contemporary world community—that is, a situation embracing different conceptions of world public order, corresponding to the different ideological blocs or groupings. And it seeks to find the "living-law" international law of today in the complex of specific accords, agreements, arrangements and *de facto* juridical relations between those different ideological groupings. This distinctively Soviet conception of world public order, especially as theoretically formulated in terms of the Legal Principles of Peaceful Coexistence, has, of course, its own built-in elements of a priori Marxist dogma and philosophical absolutism. Nevertheless, in its starting point —the plural nature of the contemporary world community—it begins with an empirical fact; and the empirical or existential has been highly influential in its concrete implementation by Soviet policy makers in direct Soviet-United States confrontations in concrete situations.

In immediate political-institutional terms, this distinctive Soviet approach has meant a denial that the United Nations Charter is the constitution of a new system of world government, to be interpreted broadly and beneficially in the sense originally advanced by Chief Justice John Marshall of the United States Supreme Court. The Charter is, in Soviet eyes, not a constitution but a treaty. As a treaty, and in accordance with general doctrinal positions on the law of treaties developed by Soviet jurists—sponsored in particular by the Soviet legal spokesmen in the detailed scientific discussions in the International Law Commission that culminated in the recent (Vienna) Convention on the Law of Treaties—the Charter is to be limited to the original historical purposes of its drafters. Also, as a treaty, it is to be interpreted strictly, even restrictively, in the fashion in which English judges traditionally interpreted statutes encroaching upon the common law. It is not for nothing that the Soviet judge, Judge Koretsky—a jurist in his own right, by the way, independently of his nomination to the World Court—agreed with that arch "strict constructionist" and disciple of Felix Frankfurter, Sir Percy Spender, in the essential principle of the majority opinion of the World Court, though not joining it in the actual final vote, in the *South-West Africa* case in 1966; and that Judge Koretsky dissented, with his Polish colleague Judge Winiarski (and also the French judge and two other Western judges), in the *Advisory Opinion on U.N. Expenses* in 1962—on "strict construction" grounds.

This Soviet position has also meant denial of any role for the U.N. General Assembly as a sort of world legislature. The Soviet Union has not merely always denied any law-making authority to the so-called "Uniting for Peace Resolution" of the U.N. General Assembly, adopted in the Korean crisis in 1951. It seems also, even in recent years when the erstwhile comfortably pro-Western voting majorities in the General Assembly have disappeared with the expansion of the United Nations to well-nigh universal membership, to have resisted the temptation to try to consolidate or institutionalize an "anticolonialist" and hence, it is argued, inevitably anti-Western and pro-Soviet voting line-up in the General Assembly. Soviet pronouncements on the legal efficacy of U.N. General Assembly Resolutions are far more cautious, reserved, and even skeptical than much of the writing by Western, and even Eastern European (other than the Soviet Union) writers. The Soviet position in the United Nations has been consistently to insist on the political and legal primacy of the Security Council in which, of course, the big power veto principle operates.

On the World Court and on the principle of judicial settlement of disputes—indeed on the principle of third-party arbitration of disputes in general—the Soviet attitude has been consistently negative. Soviet internal law—in company with that of most Continental European civil law countries, and indeed some common law countries like England—denies any general right of judicial legislation or judicial policy making. Soviet legal thinking goes beyond this to deny, in institutional terms, the possibility of an "impartial" third-party settlement—a position, by the way, somewhat ruefully accepted by the British Foreign Office in the last half of the nineteenth century after Great Britain had consistently lost a series of frontier disputes involving the then colony of Canada and the United States, which had been arbitrated by the German Emperor as a "neutral" third-party arbitrator. "Do we give up the disputed territory immediately to the United States, or do we give it up after arbitration?" ran the wry British Foreign Office joke of the time. The intrinsically technical civil law-based opposition to judicial policy making, revealed in the Soviet opposition to any activist, law-making role for the World Court, is reinforced by the Soviet institutionally based hostility to any expansionist role for the United Nations in general. But this Soviet opposition has gained strength also by the simple political fact of life, up to the present, of the underrepresentation, in voting power on the World Court, of the Soviet Union and its principal allies. Being until recently decisively outnumbered in the General Assembly and the Security Council—the two electoral colleges for the World Court—the Soviet Union and its allies have generally been a small minority —two judges out of fifteen—on the Court. Thus the Soviet Union and its allies would hardly have been in a position to influence or determine the substantive content of the "policy" in judicial policy making by the Court even if they could have brought themselves to accept such judicial policy making in principle.

With an invariably hostile attitude toward departure from the strict letter of the Charter or from the known historical intentions of its drafters, the Soviet Union could hardly have been expected to be sympathetic to the attempts by U.N. Secretary-General Dag Hammarskjöld to expand his office into an activist, executive policy-making organ. The Soviet opposition here is manifested most strikingly in its intransigent position in the crisis over U.N. expenses (in which, let it not be forgotten, it was joined also by France), and in its attempt to replace the Hammarskjöld-style "activist" Secretary-Generalship by a troika plan that would represent the Soviet, Western, and Third worlds equally, and presumably be subject to the veto of any one of them. These particular Soviet attitudes toward the United Nations are both readily understandable in terms of past Soviet historical experience with international organization in general, and also explicable in pragmatic, experiential terms having regard to prevailing power line-ups in the world community. Beginning with the old League of Nations, which Soviet writers saw from the beginning (and perhaps, in historical retrospect, with some justice) as an instrument of Western European imperialism designed primarily to institutionalize the political consequences of the Carthaginian Peace Treaty of 1919 and its Eastern European (post-Russian Revolution) analogues, Soviet jurists have always had a profound skepticism if not outright mistrust of international organizations in which their own (voting) role is doomed to be a minority one. The pusillanimous performance of the Western European family compact that dominated the old League of Nations—in regard to collective security measures intended to preserve the world balance of power that the Western European powers had themselves so largely created—against Japan in Manchuria in 1931, and then against Italy in Ethiopia in 1935, hardly increased Soviet confidence in the long-range utility of the League. The League's signal failure to do anything to check Hitler's quest for *Lebensraum* in Central Europe, followed by the League's dying gesture in the expulsion of Russia because of its frontier war with Finland in 1939–1940, completed the Soviet picture of a hypocritical, double standard of law and morality, as applied by that first institutional venture in world public order and government.

The Soviet Union, of course, had participated actively in the preliminary, private big-power meetings, and then in the 1945 San Francisco conference, which led to the formation of the United Nations. The built-in institution of the big-power veto in the

Security Council was one instrument intended to protect Soviet special interests, especially with the strong weighting of effective political power, under the United Nations Charter, in favor of the Security Council at the expense of the General Assembly. In the General Assembly itself, intended, as it was in Soviet eyes, as a purely subordinate institution, an extra sop to the Soviet Union's sensitivities as to its inevitable minority status in terms of voting alignments was provided by the separate representation (together with separate votes in the General Assembly) of the two Soviet constituent republics of Byelorussia and the Ukraine. Nevertheless, from the founding of the United Nations, and with the quick collapse of the World War II victors' own limited consensus of 1945, the Soviet Union saw its policy options reduced to the maintenance of a defensive holding operation—through the medium of the veto—in the Security Council, and to the playing of a largely impotent role in a General Assembly politically dominated, as the General Assembly effectively was until the 1956 "package deal" opened the floodgates to new members, by a pro-Western majority composed of a working coalition of the United States, the "old" (Western) commonwealth countries, Western Europe, and the twenty-one Latin American states. This was the era, of course, of the Uniting for Peace Resolution, rammed through the General Assembly by the triumphant pro-Western coalition during the Korean crisis in 1951. It was not until the late 1950's, by which time the proliferation of U.N. membership had eroded away the comfortable pro-Western majority and introduced a new fluidity and unpredictability in U.N. General Assembly voting, that the opportunity for Soviet improvisation and experimentation with an activist, adventurist, "Socialist," foreign policy in the U.N. arena was for the first time presented. By that time, of course, the old-line Stalinist authority had been overthrown within the Soviet Union itself and a new flexibility had entered into Soviet policies at home and abroad, involving also the possibility of a new flexibility in Soviet-Western relations, in place of the old rigidities of the earlier, cold war era.

In contrast to Soviet attitudes to the United Nations which were essentially negative right from the beginning, the United

174 SOVIET AND AMERICAN POLICIES IN THE UNITED NATIONS

States' original conceptions were both optimistic and expansionist, resting on the dual confidence not merely of an assured pro-Western voting majority in all main U.N. organs (including the World Court), but also, and more importantly, on a certain wave of idealistic thinking in the United States, both during and after World War II, as to the possibilities of building a better world through the methods and techniques of rationalized constitutionalism.

To outside observers, even those who are also from predominantly English-speaking, common law legal systems, the most intriguing aspect of American thinking with regard to international law has always been the coexistence of the pragmatist and the natural law strains—or the simultaneous apprehension of the elements of American self-interest present in particular legal solutions for international problems, and longer range and more comprehensive goals of world public order that might outweigh the national self-interest in the choice of one legal option rather than another solution of a given international conflict.

It has always seemed to me that this more long-range philosophic conception of the need to create a viable system of world public order, with its obvious historical debts to Woodrow Wilson's Fourteen Points, to Secretary of State Frank Kellog's pact to outlaw war (Kellogg-Briand Peace Pact), and to Wendell Willkie's "One World," was the dominant element in American planning in the early period of the United Nations, roughly from 1945 until the outbreak of the Korean conflict in 1950. Wishful thinking of American leaders of the period is reflected in the rather simplistic projection into the world community of institutional forms drawn from American internal, or municipal, constitutional law, as if—to paraphrase President Eisenhower's Secretary of the Defense's later remark, "What is good for General Motors is good for the country!"—what works within the special legal community of the contemporary United States must automatically work when translated into the far broader and far different world community. The genesis of the philosophical conception of the U.N. General Assembly as an all-powerful, all-embracing, superlegislature—a conception taken up in recent years in some of the new Afro-Asian countries—is to be found in this same era of American legal thinking; just as is the conception of the World Court as a legislating, policy-making tribunal on the lines of the United States Supreme Court. The latter conception, by the way, emerges rather oddly from American thinking, when we consider the highly defensive, American approach to acceptance of the compulsory jurisdiction of the World Court through the device of the Connally Amendment. I think it may have come as something of a surprise and a disappointment to American leaders of the immediate postwar era that their enthusiasm and high hopes for the embryonic United Nations organization were hardly shared, not merely by the Soviet Union but also by the United States' main Western allies. The explanation for the lack of enthusiasm of the Western allies, and particularly the Europeans, for the United Nations is to be found, I think, in a certain time-lag between American and European thinking on constitutional forms and institutions, and on the limits of law generally in controlling societal tensions, whether national or international.

The period between the two World Wars was the period par excellence of European faith in rationalized constitutionalism and in the attempt to control power through paper affirmations. It was the period of constitution making—of elaborate drafts with poetic preambles, of separation and balancing of governmental institutions, and of fine sounding Bills of Rights. Yet, in the end these legal philosophers' drafts were impotent to control the onset of Fascism, and minority rights and claims were ruthlessly trampled on despite the poetic eloquence of the constitutional guarantees and formal protections. It is not surprising that after 1945 European constitutionalists felt a certain cynicism, born of their own bitter experiences between the two World Wars, in regard to the American leaders' high hopes for the United Nations. A dominant, law-making, U.N. General Assembly, in which every country was accorded an equal vote, would run counter to the elemental constitutional principle of the necessary minimum relation between law and power, quite apart from the obvious damage it would do to the post-1945 victors' balance of power which rested on the wartime minimum consensus between the Soviet and United States and Western allies. As for a policy-making World Court, that conception not only ran directly counter to the dominant

legal attitudes and experience of the main Western countries apart
from the United States, whether common law or civil law, quite
apart from the Soviet Union, but also, when presented as a
constitutional absolute that purportedly was good for all seasons,
it ignored the basic fact that not all international problem-
situations are ripe for solution by legal, and specifically by
judicial, means. Indeed, it may be argued that the history of the
World Court itself, since its reconstitution after 1945, demonstrates that a legal solution, because of the air of infallibility and
finality with which judgment is rendered in favor of one side
only of the problem at issue, may sometimes seriously delay or
impede a rational political solution to the dispute which would
normally proceed by way of bargain and, ultimately, compromise.
The World Court's advisory opinion of 1962 on *U.N. Expenses*
is perhaps the most striking example of this proposition. The
handing down of the World Court's Opinion led directly to the
United States-sponsored show-down in the U.N. General Assembly, with the United States attempting to apply article 19 of the
U.N. Charter to take away the Soviet vote (and also the French
vote) in the General Assembly as long as the special dues remained
unpaid. This tactical move had the direct result of bringing the
work of the nineteenth session of the General Assembly in the Fall
of 1964 to a standstill; and the resultant U.N. political crisis was
not resolved until twelve months later when the United States
finally backed down, allowing the work of the succeeding, twentieth session of the General Assembly to proceed without resolving
the *U.N. Expenses* issue.

I think there is a perceptible change in the attitude of American decision makers toward the United Nations, beginning perhaps with the Korean crisis and the successful vote of the U.N.
Security Council taken in the absence of the Soviet representative
and with the Uniting for Peace Resolution passed by the U.N.
General Assembly. American self-interest comes to be emphasized
more openly, and there is concomitantly a much more frank and
public acceptance of the principle of maximizing one's own tactical
political advantages in confrontations with the Soviet Union and
the Soviet bloc generally in all specialized arenas of the United
Nations. This new dominant current in American legal thinking

may be regarded as having been established with Secretary of State Dean Acheson's growing and well-publicized disenchantment with the United Nations as a rational forum for decision making on intense international issues. This disenchantment brought with it, I think, a certain element of detachment or disengagement from practice of the U.N.-"One World" type thinking, and a new tendency to regard the arenas, institutions, and procedures for settlement of disputes as necessarily subordinate to the actual settlement itself. This is an intellectual attitude and outlook that survived through Secretary of State Dulles' era, with its absolutistic Natural Law-type undertones of an American mission to "roll back Communist Imperialism," and on to President Kennedy's term when the contemporary United States positions and general philosophy toward the United Nations may be said to have been developed or confirmed.

. . . . .

Looking back at both Soviet and American attitudes toward the United Nations since its founding in 1945, I think it may be said that the Soviet attitudes tend to reveal a rather greater degree of consistency and long-range purpose. The initial Soviet skepticism toward the United Nations and denial of any world state role for it, born of bitter Soviet experience and a recognition of the original, post-1945, political facts-of-life that assured the Soviet Union's hopelessly minority status within the United Nations and its main organs, survived into the era of the "new" United Nations, commencing with the late 1950's and early 1960's, when the proliferation of U.N. membership clearly would have facilitated the Soviet Union's building of a determinedly "anti-Colonialist," anti-Western, coalition in the U.N. The Soviet Union signally failed to profit from Western embarrassments at that time. This may have been because (in Dewey's terms) there was in the Soviet Union a terminal value in the old legal ideas and because the Soviet Foreign Ministry simply had not realized how much the change in U.N. membership had dated their own old stereotypes of a defensive, holding attitude toward the U.N. Or else, more imaginatively, it was because Soviet jurists accepted the principle that their long-range interests as a big power —and one of the two major nuclear powers at that—dictated a generally reserved, negative, attitude toward the United Nations as a peacekeeping agency, thus dictating also a continuance of the main elements of the Soviet Union's general, post-1945, policy toward the United Nations.

The interesting thing in the present context is that, starting with radically different a priori philosophical and tactical premises, the United States seems now to have ended up with something very close to the Soviet Union's special position vis-à-vis the United Nations, this perhaps as a long-range consequence of the ending of the cold war, and of the achievement of the Soviet-American détente with the peaceful resolution of the Cuban missile crisis of October 1962.

We may sum up the main elements of this Soviet-United States *de facto* accord as to the role of the United Nations before proceeding to consider its implications for the future of the United Nations and of its main organs.

First, both the Soviet Union and the United States seem now agreed that the United Nations is not a suitable arena for the negotiation or settlement of the really serious conflicts in contemporary international relations; and they seem agreed that to bring such conflicts to the United Nations—at least before they are finally resolved—may actually harm the process of big power adjustment and compromise and thus delay or impede dispute settlement altogether. Thus it is that key issues like the Cuban missile crisis of 1962, the achievement of a ban on nuclear testing in 1963, the attempts at settlement of the Vietnam War and of the continuing Middle Eastern conflict, are either not brought to the United Nations at all, or, if so, are brought there only after settlement—as a polite afterthought or for the sake of protocol. The approved medium of settlement of such key issues is direct, bilateral, Soviet-United States negotiation; and the preferred arena for resolution of Soviet-United States conflicts thus becomes the summit meeting *à deux,* far from the noise and distraction, the incidental playing to the gallery, and, in the end, the sheer political irrelevance in big-power terms of the U.N. General Assembly with its multitude of new members and ministates whose voting rights are quite unrelated to their political power.

Second, even where the Soviet Union and the United States accept to negotiate within the framework of the United Nations, —as with Disarmament; or in the context of a multilateral treaty, —as with Space problems, the operational methodology for achievement of the final settlement will be direct, bilateral Soviet-United States negotiations. The Soviet and United States delegations may be expected to consult constantly and exchange drafts of the proposed treaty or convention until, finally, substantive identity is achieved between their two proposals. In effect, the other countries will be presented with the final draft on a take-it-or-leave-it basis. This, in fact, is what was done, quite crudely, with the Moscow Test Ban Treaty of August 1963: it was worked out and adopted by the Soviet Union and the United States (and Great Britain) and then presented to the rest of the world for signature, without, however, extending any right on the part of other countries to alter or modify the three-power text. With other drafts approved by the Soviet Union and the United States, like the Moon Treaty of January 1967, and the nonproliferation treaty project, the methods have been a little more veiled perhaps, but the original Soviet-United States "club" consensus has remained as the authoritative departure point. This may explain some of the political difficulties that the nonproliferation treaty project is now having in securing general ratification.

Third, the Soviet Union seems to have decided *not* to try now to politicize unduly the process of election to the World Court. In thus resisting the temptation, especially strong in the aftermath of the Court's *South-West Africa* decision of 1966, to try to build an anti-Western coalition on the Court as a basis for a future policy-making (and, specifically, a "Socialist" policy-making) role for the Court, Soviet policy makers have acted consistently with past Soviet doctrinal attitudes toward the Court. It must be said, in fact, that the Soviet approach to the World Court to date has tended to be dignified and restrained. Though political factors have clearly been paramount considerations in the choice of Soviet candidates for election to the Court, not less perhaps than is true of some of the Western candidates also, Soviet judges on the World Court have tended to have intellectual calibre in their own right as legal scientists, apart from their appointment to the Court. In particular, Judge Koretsky, in the *cause célèbre* of the *South-West Africa* case, though dissenting from the majority opinion of Sir Percy Spender, seemed at pains to eschew polemics in passing up a seeming golden opportunity to take cheap political debating points against the West. Judge Koretsky's dissenting opinion in the *South-West Africa* case is, in fact, a model of technical legal craftsmanship and of prudent economy of style and drafting. Judge Koretsky himself has preferred to explain the judicial philosophy reflected in his dissenting opinion as an example of the acceptance of the principle of collegial responsibility and the respect that any one member of a court, even a dissenting judge, owes to his colleagues. This is an approach that is fully consistent with general civil law (and not less with Russian civil law) conceptions of the judicial process and of the role of the individual judge in a multimember court, apart from its conformance to long-range Soviet attitudes toward the World Court and to judicially based law making in the international arena generally.

As for the U.S. viewpoint, it must be said that the United States now shows no great hurry to rush into court for settlement of its major disputes and disagreements with the Soviet Union. The proposals by Secretary of State William P. Rogers to the American Society of International Law Annual Meeting, in April 1970, for encouraging increased resort to the World Court could, on this view, apply to the secondary or relatively trivial international disputes, and not to the really major high-tension issues of international relations today, a fact that Secretary Rogers himself recognizes in conceding explicitly that "no international legal order, however restructured, is likely to solve many of the major disputes involving issues of war and peace." In fact, in the long range, we seem to have a tacit acceptance by the United States of the merits of the Soviet position—amply voiced in the United Nations Sixth (Legal) Committee, in the United Nations General Assembly's Special Committee on Friendly Relations, and indeed in Soviet juristic literature generally—that judicial settlement is only one among a number of different modes of dispute settlement, that it has no special claims to hierarchical superiority to the other modes of settlement, and that, in general, direct diplomatic negotiations are the most operationally productive mode of dispute settlement in a world community characterized by deep-set ideological divisions and conflicts. It is significant that the long-range Soviet distaste for the World Court has now been reinforced not merely by the bitter Afro-Asian reaction to the *South-West Africa* decision, but also most recently by the manifest irritation of certain Continental European foreign ministries and their national legal establishments at the "gratuitous interventions" by some of the non-Continental European judges in what was, in origin, a purely Continental European "family compact" dispute involving only West Germany, Denmark, and The Netherlands—the *North Sea Continental Shelf* cases of 1969. Truly, the cause of judicial law making and judicial policy making at the international level is at a very low ebb at the present time, with the World Court having no cases at all now remaining on its docket although the world community continues to be beset by a plethora of unresolved problems!

Fourth, and with particular reference to the United Nations' specialized agencies, the Soviet Union and the United States seem agreed, after their experience with the U.N. General Assembly in recent years, that the principle of mathematical equality of voting power is not a rational one, at least where special obligations, commitments, or expenditures are demanded of the big powers. In these cases, the Soviet and the United States seem agreed on the merits of reproducing, in measure, the Security Council principle of weighted voting, the weighting according in measure with the special big-power interests and responsibilities. Thus UNCTAD (the United Nations Conference on Trade and Development) has followed the International Monetary Fund principle of according a specially favored voting position to the big powers, in direct relation to their disproportionately heavy financial responsibilities.

Fifth, both the Soviet Union and the United States can be expected to continue to view with reserve, or certainly with less than downright enthusiasm, the pretensions of some of the current activist group in the U.N. General Assembly to a law-making role that is supposedly inherent in the General Assembly. It is significant that the juristic writing that argues for such a norm-making competence inhering in the General Assembly is predominantly from the Third World or else from the supporting (satellite) countries of Eastern Europe. The Soviet juristic literature on the subject is appropriately guarded and tends to hedge its bets. The American official position in recent years has tended, reciprocally, to play down the legal value or utility of vague general resolutions adopted in the General Assembly, full of sound and fury and signifying nothing of an immediately concrete or operational character. The United States has also tended increasingly either to abstain on final votes on such resolutions or even to vote against such resolutions altogether.

.   .   .   .   .

It seems to me that the Soviet Union and the United States, responding directly to their own national self-interest, have arrived by pragmatic, empirical, problem-oriented, step-by-step methods at very much the same basic conclusions in regard to the United Nations. Each seems to have concluded that the business of world peacekeeping is far too serious to be left to the United Nations proper, and that they must, therefore, jointly assume responsibility for it. In place of the old bipolar, hostile confrontation of the cold war era, we thus seem to have a sort of Soviet-United States consensus as to the basic arrangements and conditions of world public order, paralleling the old Concert of Europe or Holy Alliance of the post-1815 Europe that was shaped by the Congress of Vienna.

Whether such a "gentlemen's agreement" between the Soviet and the United States—the Balance of Nuclear Responsibility, as it has been called, in place of the old Balance of Nuclear Terror, or, as I have described it in another context, the *Pax Metternichea*—can survive indefinitely in a world community that has seen the condition of bipolarity give way to polypolarity, with the outright Byzantinism within the old NATO alliance on the one hand and the schism between Communist China and the

Soviet Union on the other, is open to question. What is clear, however, is that as long as this special understanding between the Soviet and the United States survives politically, it is likely to provide at least a viable base for minimum world peacekeeping. This indeed has been demonstrated empirically, in the years since the détente was first achieved, with the peaceful resolution of the Cuban missile crisis in October 1962. By the same token, the United Nations is likely to continue to be, as it has been during those years of the détente, at best a subordinate, ancillary instrument for peacekeeping and for international problem solving generally, with the really important problems of contemporary international relations, however, reserved for decision or compromise in other arenas, and with a continuous search for new institutional machinery for peacekeeping outside of the formal United Nations network. This continuing emphasis and trend in contemporary international law and relations may not be very good for the health of the United Nations organization, of course, but it may still provide a most useful and productive, and ultimately realistic, approach to minimum peacekeeping in the politically divided, ideologically pluralist, world community of the present era.

POSTSCRIPT OR PROLOGUE?

George Ginsburgs
and
Alvin Z. Rubinstein

The policies pursued by the Soviet Union and the United States in the United Nations have been fundamentally symmetrical and have had similar consequences. As the preceding essays amplify, the superpowers have sought to carry on their global competition and occasional accommodation independent of the United Nations, and often at the expense of the U.N. as an institution and of its constituent members. National interests, not international concerns, have dictated their behavior in the world organization. Neither superpower ever considered subordinating its perceived national aims to any voting constellation of lesser states, a truism woven integrally into the fabric of the U.N. Charter by the inclusion of the veto power; neither ever intended to forego the promotion of its imperium. But both clearly have adapted to respond in more sophisticated fashion to the changing character of the U.N. system, a development they did not foresee, desire, nor nurture, yet one, paradoxically, they dare not ignore.

Any discussion of the relations between the Soviet Union, the United States, and the United Nations inevitably starts from the alpha element of power, defined as the sum of each party's ability to impose its will on one or both of the other parties in the triangular association, and conceived as a dynamic quality which may vary markedly, depending on the time frame, the agenda issue, or the salience of extraneous factors. Universal equations that would give expression to this process and account for every contingency have so far turned out to be either too comprehensive for operational application in specific instances or platitudinous in the sense of producing self-evident explications that any semi-informed observer could readily have arrived at by virtue of common sense alone. A sample of "archetypal" cases may thus prove more useful in ascertaining the limits to the freedom of initiative enjoyed by the members of our cast in pursuing their policy objectives in concert with or in opposition to one another. Three types of situations may be singled out for attention: in the first, the superpowers monopolize the substantive issues and can seemingly arrange matters to suit themselves, yet their behavior is not unaffected by U.N. pressures; in the second, the United Nations produces a signal achievement which, on closer examination, could not have been carried out without a measure of superpower passivity and benevolence; and in the third situation, the superpowers appropriate an international issue raised under U.N. aegis, and in the process transform the discussion to one involving their own national interests.

Like everyone else, we begin by recognizing the obvious discrepancy in the quantum of physical power at the disposal of the United States and the Soviet Union, on the one hand, and the United Nations, on the other. What this means is that the United Nations will never be in a position, as long as this state of affairs exists, to dictate its own wishes to the superpowers jointly or severally. In principle, however, the reverse is quite possible for in a bilateral confrontation between the United Nations and the United States or the Soviet Union, either of the latter can command a preponderance of military strength presumably adequate to achieve its ends.

Here we have essentially the kind of situation that obtains in the matter of nuclear arms control, in which the interests of the Soviet Union and the United States seem to be in open contradiction with the expectations of the majority of the international community which is represented in the United Nations and sets the tone for the organization's pronouncements on this item of the agenda. Using a power-oriented frame of reference, one is compelled to admit that the United Nations cannot, in the prevailing circumstances, hope to alter the views of the U.S.S.R. or the United States in this sphere, assuming a strong commitment on the part of the latter to a fixed course of action. To a devotee of the United Nations as an aspiring world government, to a champion of the formula that mankind's salvation lies in the capacity of the international forum to prescribe norms of conduct for all nations without exception, the prospect must indeed look grim and with cause. A jaundiced glance at the scenario then leads to the usual lament that the superpowers do as they please and either disregard the United Nations or settle their business in camera and only afterwards invite the United Nations to append its signature to the document without exercising the privilege of criticizing or revising the contents.

Granted that in a duel-like contest, the outcome is predictable. For all that, the picture just drawn leaves one with the uncomfortable feeling that it is too pat and simplistic. To begin with, the United Nations as a collective entity need not accede to any scheme worked out by the two principals should it find itself in serious disagreement, and by demurring it can refuse to legitimize the project. Although this may not prevent Moscow and Washington from going ahead with the proposal anyway, chances of their electing to buck the quasi-unanimous opinion of the global assembly are slight and the result is much more likely to be a scramble to discover ways of composing the differences and forging a mutually acceptable compromise plan. In fact, the incipient emergence of a substantial dissenting faction would probably be enough to spark a drive to build a wider consensus through accommodations that would narrow the gap among the diverse groups, eventually creating the proper middle ground to permit a meeting of the minds of most participants. Under ordinary conditions, the desire for general approbation provides a greater incentive for making requisite adjustments than any countervailing impulse to preserve the language of the original draft. To be sure, exceptions are known to occur—France and China have not ratified the test-ban treaty; the nonproliferation pact too has run into its share of abstentions—and this has ob-

viously engendered a certain amount of international malaise as
to the ultimate value of a convention to which various important
states will not subscribe.

The dissidents are not many, though, and when the other
side includes the dominant nuclear powers plus the vast majority
of the international community, the notion that four-fifths of a
loaf of bread is superior to none carries considerable weight and
generates the impetus to bring the enterprise to fruition. This
is not to say that the arms control situation escapes the effects of
the chronic tension between the "haves" and the "have nots"
or that the quest for a *modus vivendi* is devoid of rivalry. A priori
divergences of attitude are by no means eliminated, but are
transcended by (*a*) the perceived urgency to bind the nuclear
giants to a designated code of behavior which, while perhaps not
perfect, is infinitely preferable to a legal vacuum in which everyone improvises his own traffic regulations and lethal collisions are
all but inevitable, (*b*) the appreciation of the immense disparity
between the rights and duties of the members of the nonnuclear
club which puts them at a terrible disadvantage in pushing demands since they have very little to offer in *quid pro quo*.

If that is true of the terminal stage, the description fits the
preliminary phase equally well. It is all too easily forgotten that
from the outset the impetus for establishing some degree of arms
control came from the smaller states while the main contenders for
world supremacy seemed bent on piling up the largest possible
storehouse of sophisticated weaponry. The specific idea of a reduction in the size, or at least a moratorium on the further growth,
of the arsenal actually originated with the lesser powers who—
unable either to keep up with the race or counter it—found their
very survival imperiled by the proliferation of means of mass destruction the use of which hinged on the decision of just a few
individuals preoccupied, quite naturally, with their own national
interests rather than those of third parties. The ensuing deluge
of studies, position papers, exploratory surveys, conferences and
colloquia, informal discussions and private talks, ventures into
personal diplomacy, trial balloons, hortatory resolutions, draft proposals adds up to a vast drive to educate the global constituency

in the dangers of unlimited military investment much on the pattern of pressure group politics.

Besides urging the superpowers to recognize the dangers of letting military research and production run riot, through their persistent efforts the architects of the various campaigns for international curbs on military technology attained a dual goal: (*a*) they cultivated in people everywhere the belief that effective measures of arms control were feasible, a sentiment that in turn made itself felt on the domestic scene and bred a psychological predisposition in favor of at least exploring the possibilities of checking a headlong rush toward oblivion; (*b*) more important, they gradually fostered the realization within official circles in Washington and Moscow that there were areas in which one could conceivably experiment with projects entailing a modicum of physical self-restraint without irrevocably jeopardizing national security. Clearly, obsessed as they were with their particular images of the international political environment, neither the Soviet nor the American hierarchy was likely to reach these conclusions by itself and the fact that they had been independently formulated in quarters not associated with the "enemy" only enhanced their attractiveness.

To the extent, then, that recently some progress has been made in this matter, a great deal of credit for getting the job done goes, *ultima ratio,* to the nonaligned element within the United Nations, often large enough to usurp the institution's voice and promote it as its own, which sustained this unparalleled cycle of agitation and enlightenment among both citizens and governments and succeeded in pinpointing sundry items on which a practical concordance could be, and in some cases has since been, achieved. By mapping the terrain, advertising certain principles and ideas until they almost triggered conditioned reflexes, the groundwork was laid for the tentative détente and rapprochement which we now see in a number of sectors pertaining to the development and future deployment of new weapons systems.

To be sure, some analysts maintain that these are marginal gains, fringe benefits that do not affect the hard core of the immense military programs that continued unabated in the United

States and the Soviet Union. Whether that is so or not, concrete evidence that agreement can be arrived at in isolated instances holds out hope of other such breakthroughs, the cumulative impact of which might start mankind on the road back from the brink of nuclear extermination. Constructive egotism nurtured by pragmatic experience could in the end bring these things to pass faster than any elaborate vision of a transfigured world or human metamorphosis. If that should happen, we will be heavily indebted to the patient and arduous labor of the administrative staff and state component of the U.N. for pulling the scattered pieces together and fitting them into a meaningful script to convey a positive message even to regimes blinded by hatred, fear, and megalomania.

One should not be ungrateful to the superpowers for steps they have recently initiated to improve the arms picture. Nevertheless, it does seem pertinent to emphasize that while their rather arrogant demeanor in spelling out the terms of the *modus vivendi* without consulting their colleagues in the United Nations obscures all they owe the latter for simply being in shape to carry out the enterprise and feed the cynical view of a Soviet-American *diktat* to the rest of the international community, basically this conveys a false impression. Though the technical details of the arrangements are, without a doubt, of Soviet-American provenance as is the crucial decision to give the venture a try, the faith and inspiration that saw the ship safely into port emanated from other sources and the final product emerges as humanity's brainchild and not just a private offshoot of a casual Russian-American liaison.

Let us now look at the reverse situation—the phenomenon of decolonization—which is commonly alleged to have taken place without the participation and assistance of the two major powers. As one might surmise, the above characterization is only half accurate. Undeniably, neither the United States nor the Soviet Union exerted any direct influence on the struggle for independence waged by the colonial and semicolonial nations after the close of World War II. In part, this "neutrality" may well have been due simply to a spell of shortsightedness in responsible quarters in Moscow and Washington: obsessed with the cold war, the arms race, and the East–West rift, both capitals may literally have overlooked the explosive potential of the anti-imperialist tide, a somewhat ironic commentary on their powers of perception since the Americans and the Russians may on this occasion have shown themselves to be equally incapable of appreciating the mood of the times and similarly ill-attuned to the hopes and aspirations of the bulk of mankind. Utterly fascinated by each other, the leaders of the U.S.S.R. and the United States tended to brush aside the universal cry for national self-rule as a secondary matter when compared with their titanic match for global dominion, largely oblivious of the paradoxical fact that the eventual destruction of the old empires would do more to change the map of the earth, the flavor of international diplomacy, and the complexion of the United Nations than all their ponderous maneuvers vis-à-vis to gain the upper hand. In part, however, both were also prisoners of circumstances that sharply limited their freedom of action and relegated them to an essentially passive role while the flood peaked and then began subsiding.

Without foreign possessions of their own, the Americans and the Russians escaped the personal travails of the decolonization experience. Next, the United States had to take into account that the principal colonial states involved in the current drama were meanwhile its staunchest allies in the postwar defense system aimed at containing the threat of Communist expansion, so that although various U.S. administrations may have felt little sympathy for colonialism, this aversion could not be expressed in a way that would alienate or weaken France or Great Britain, for example, to a point where they ceased to be useful as political and military partners altogether. Perhaps it was impossible in practice to prevent American financial and military subsidies from being siphoned off into vain attempts to suppress the liberation movements in assorted corners of the French and British empires, but Washington's lack of enthusiasm for the perpetuation of the *status quo* guaranteed that such diversion would be minimal and consist of surpluses that could be spared from the primary job of manning Europe's front lines. The flow was not stopped; yet it was substantially reduced from the size it might otherwise have assumed had the United States wholeheartedly backed the metropolitan powers in a scheme to preserve their overseas holdings intact.

There is no getting around the ambivalence of the American position in this context; still, Washington did manage to stay officially uncommitted and retain a degree of balance and objectivity in the face of unfolding events so as not to become a captive of its friends in the pursuit of their private feuds. Given the temper of the epoch, this was no mean feat, all criticisms to the contrary notwithstanding, for the pressure very definitely ran in the direction of standing by our traditional companions in their hour of need despite our historical identification with the principle of self-determination.

The Russians faced no such dilemma. They were physically precluded from immixing themselves in the anticolonial struggle by geographical distance, ignorance of native conditions, and absence of local contacts. They could and did offer moral support, rhetorical encouragement, and unsolicited advice, but had neither the opportunity, nor the logistical means, nor, probably, the desire to sit in on the game. Most analysts stress the first element in the equation and too easily forget that the Russians may also have had a positive motive in staying in the background and that is not to provoke an American intervention which the Soviets could not hope to counter effectively and which would mean that the revolutionary regime in the dependent territory would henceforth have to contend with American power, incomparably superior to that of the original colonial master, and be doomed to failure or compelled to adopt a pro-American coloration and orientation.

Thus, in the end what we have is not a static tableau in which the United States and the Soviet Union are depicted as either totally unaware of the dynamic quality of the decolonization process or frankly disinterested in its achievements, but a relationship pregnant with tension, purposeful intent, and a spirit of active competition which had a radical impact on the outcome of the contest. Because of Moscow's and Washington's overt ideological opposition to prewar colonialism, the anti-imperialist forces had to cope with only second-echelon powers; the scale was not weighted entirely in favor of one adversary and the challenger now gained a good chance of success. In addition, both the United States and the U.S.S.R. advocated the emancipation of the colonies and sought by sundry methods to propagate that thesis, the United States trusting that its allies would accept its views and relinquish their domains abroad in a peaceful manner, the U.S.S.R. trying to profit from the situation by championing the anticolonial cause and depriving its chief capitalist enemies of an important source of strength and wealth.

Finally, the realization that any initiative by one party automatically furnished entry to the other and fear of the consequences of a confrontation in the highly volatile atmosphere of a political milieu with which neither was familiar convinced the antagonists that a watchful vigil from the edges of the arena, thereby offsetting each other's presence and negating each other's shadow, served their goals better than a combat assignment. Where the rule has been violated, as in the Congo affair, by a wild swing to the left or to the right, even if engineered solely by a corps of local actors, the superpowers have felt impelled to take steps to redress the balance. Short of this, they have been content to play the part of observers and referees while the opposing teams vying in the junior league settled the score. Contrary to what is usually asserted, this does not spell impotence or apathy. Rather, for good reason, Moscow and Washington from the first reached the conclusion that direct interference in the colonialist struggle was not desirable and that they could do more by monitoring the events and supplying a mutual antidote. Nevertheless, by remote control, so to speak, they fixed the parameters of the conflict, dictated the acceptable style, and by inference suggested the basic outlines of a viable solution. This smacks less of indifference than of a conscious experiment in low-key rivalry within a common framework designed to maintain the general equilibrium. The U.N. may be the most visible and vocal member of the cast, but it is still a three-handed match.

If at the extremes the operation resembles a dialectical synthesis, the intermediate range of options is a straight blend, except that the choice of procedures will often determine the roles performed by the diverse factions in drafting the subsequent scenario. The Maltese proposal for the internationalization of the ocean bed, explored in the preceding pages, is an excellent illustration of how the primordial formulation of a project can affect its future fate by stipulating the radius of the problem, the circle of participants, and the conceptual foundations of the enterprise.

Articulating the scheme in global terms, as its sponsors elected to do, has the obvious advantage, of course, of dramatizing the issue and at once focusing maximum public attention on the plan's contents as well as concentrating on the elaboration of a uniform code governing the totality of the regime of the sea bed. The liabilities inherent in such an approach are that the entire family of nations is involved; every political calculation, bias, and prejudice leaves a mark on the deliberations; a vast spectrum of questions has to be examined and answered with respect to likely contingencies, side effects, reverberations in adjacent areas, etc., so that the task of forging a consensus becomes infinitely more time consuming and complicated; and the prospects of achieving success are proportionately diminished.

For all its flaws, a more modest blueprint—one geared to the practical exigencies of regional geographic units, for instance —might have met with fewer difficulties and produced faster results. On an *ad hoc*, pragmatic level, first steps have already been instituted to exploit the subsoil resources of the North Sea; the Sea of Japan is another candidate for distribution and apportionment among the respective littoral states to tap its underwater mineral riches; the Mediterranean basin awaits similar treatment. All this proceeds without reference to the universal norms that are scheduled to, and indeed some day might, be concretized in the omnibus convention currently under study. In the interim these uncoordinated and purely empirical experiments will generate their own body of rules which will have to be taken into account in drafting the final charter. In the light of the way international law and diplomacy function, it is probable that the gradual accretion of such piecemeal solutions in response to specific needs will contribute more to shaping the general agreement than any assemblage of a priori postulates *de lege ferenda* about what the status of the sea bed ideally ought to be and how it should be utilized for the benefit of all mankind, regardless of the amount of national investment in the common effort to develop these assets or even the ability to bear a significant share of the heavy expenditure called for before appreciable dividends can be earned from the venture.

Aiming for the ultimate target can thus be faulted on several grounds. One, the technique unnecessarily multiplies the obstacles to an early solution by diffusing the energies of the interested parties in a search for comprehensive prescriptions applicable to every situation and acceptable to all governments. Second, the pressure to accommodate and reconcile a plethora of divergent viewpoints renders the task of winning unanimity incomparably more complex. Third, under the circumstances, vague, catch-all provisions tend to proliferate, much to the detriment of the code's practical value as a regulator of state activities in the field. Fourth, if the process takes long enough and meanwhile various countries go ahead and stake out claims in contiguous maritime regions, a serious gap can arise between the record of *de facto* behavior and the corpus of juridical desiderata, leading to friction and confusion.

As a matter of sheer expediency, too, the move was singularly ill advised for the following reasons. The two superpowers sense no great urgency in defining at this juncture the regime of the ocean bed since neither expects soon to be dependent on this source to feed its industrial machine and so will not be stampeded into contracting a hasty deal that could adversely affect its long-range interests. The economic disparity between the smaller members of the U.N. and the superpowers is such as to deprive the former of any real bargaining weight vis-à-vis Washington and Moscow, whereas in a regional association the lag between them and the technically advanced second-echelon nations (Great Britain, Germany, Japan, France, Italy, Sweden, etc.) would not be near so overwhelming and their chances of influencing the terms of cooperation commensurately stronger. The middle-sized states with the requisite scientific knowledge and skill must constantly look for new stocks of cheaper raw materials to stay competitive in the world market against the more diversified production and service aggregates that have grown up in the United States and the Soviet Union and therefore would be more amenable to making concessions and compromises in favor of their lesser partners in exchange for guaranteed access to these enormous reservoirs of virgin wealth.

The purpose here is not to criticize the way in which the business has been handled until now, but simply to indicate that the way the initial bid is phrased makes a big difference in what occurs next; while the trio of the United States, the Soviet Union, and the United Nations is likely to occupy center stage regardless of organizational niceties, the voice each will have in the ensuing negotiations does reflect the decisions reached at the preparatory stage as to whether to slant the agenda in a particular direction. The result will invariably be in the nature of a symbiosis; yet, the precise details of the arrangement can still prove crucial for the subsequent history of the operation and its impact on the further progress of human affairs.

Given that under present conditions all concerned are committed to a policy of mutual adjustment which, to the extent possible, eschews the dramatics of confrontation and ultimata, the question remains as to how profoundly the established protocol would be altered by the seating of Red China in the forum. At first blush, the inclination might be to say that while Peking's appearance on the scene might tangentially affect the tone and style of the public transactions in the U.N. venue, few vital changes should be expected as regards matters of substance. Of course, any such exercise is bound to be speculative and a key factor in attempting to predict the consequences of China's admission to the U.N. lies in the timing of the event: the militant and ideologically intransigent China we observe today would conduct itself far differently than a potentially more tractable China of some years hence. However, for the sake of argument, let us assume that the mainland China regime that finally takes its place on the roster of U.N. members continues officially to espouse a program of world revolution. What effect is this apt to have on the U.N.'s *modus operandi?*

For one, it is clear that at the current stage if the Soviet Union and the United States either oppose or merely abstain on an item to which discussions in the United Nations are being addressed, the organization's membership will then very probably find itself without any "Great Power" leadership. Nationalist

China, Great Britain, and France, notwithstanding an occasional spark of independent spirit, are essentially client states which will not defy the will of the United States on critical issues and which in any case generally tend to agree with Washington's evaluation of modern diplomatic phenomena. By contrast, Communist China is sufficiently its own master to offer sympathy, inspiration, and support to any emerging bloc within the United Nations of countries dissenting from an attitude shared by the United States and the Soviet Union toward a problem which has been dropped in the U.N.'s lap. Such an ingredient might be instrumental in helping a majority vote to crystallize where otherwise a desultory denunciation of the Soviet-American position might be the sole response. Even if this only means impressive rhetorical fireworks, repeated polarization of this sort within the U.N. chambers would drastically transform the old rapport in the U.N.'s conference halls by emphasizing and institutionalizing the politics of conflict and spotlighting the role of numerical superiority instead of relying on consensual techniques and the virtues of broad, cross-sectional accords which blur the underlying controversies pitting East against West and the Third World against both. An adversary climate, though perhaps just of a verbal nature, would push the Soviet Union and the United States further into an isolationist frame of mind from which the United Nations would be perceived as a nuisance and an oratorical arsonist swayed by passion alone at the expense of all due sense of civic responsibility.

The outcome would entail incalculable damage to the cause of world peace and stability and set mankind back God knows how many years in its search for international law and order. Nor can the scenario be airily dismissed as the figment of an overwrought imagination if one takes trouble to note the growing rift between the "haves" and the "have nots" within U.N. circles, the disenchantment and despair of the poorer nations at the widening chasm between their rate of economic growth and average standard of living and that of their wealthier neighbors, the marked willingness to experiment with radical alternatives exhibited by the political elites of the emergent countries compared with the increasing conservatism of the United States as well as

the Soviet Union on that score and their glaring failure to al-
leviate the world's ills or sacrifice a measure of their personal
comfort to assist others.

While Communist China's tactics in the United Nations
would not, by and large, carry the risk of an escalation in the
incidence of resort to force for the reason that its military
capability is as yet very limited and will remain so in the fore-
seeable future, one can readily conceive of a situation in which,
by taking sides in a minor dispute between secondary states in
the face of a neutral stance by both superpowers, Communist
China might precipitate armed hostilities where the odds against
an outbreak of violence would have been far greater without this
element of incitement. To be sure, this would be true only of
marginal contingencies, but here China could play a role in
exacerbating international tensions and pushing a part of the
world community down the path to dangerous adventure notwithstanding the wishes and placations of Moscow and Washington. Fanning the flames of the national liberation movement in
South Africa and catering to the vengeful mood of the African
ultras in their determination to wipe out the vestiges of European
hegemony on the continent, for example, would be a test case
of Communist China's ability to outmaneuver its more orthodox
competitors and put itself at the head of the extremist fringe in
an open challenge to the United States and the Soviet Union.

Should China now manage to muster a preponderance of
backing in the ranks of the U.N. members, the split between the
"new United Nations" and the superpowers would be complete
and international relations would assume a different aspect. The
old game would be over and another would have to be devised
in its place, with suitably revised instructions on how the contenders must comport themselves, what the prize is, what constitutes
a victory, and the rest of the procedural minutiae attendant on a
carefully structured match. When that happens, the prospect of
undertaking a thorough reappraisal of many, if not most, of our
previous assumptions about the dynamics of the U.S.S.R.-U.S.A.-
U.N. *ménage à trois* will again stare us squarely in the face, a
boon to those who seek fresh worlds to conquer, a pain to those
who prefer familiar landscapes.

SELECTED BIBLIOGRAPHY

Allen, Robert Loring, "United Nations Technical Assistance: Soviet and East European Participation," *International Organization*, XI, 4 (Autumn 1957), 615–634.

Anand, R. P., "The United States and the World Court," *International Studies* (India), VI, 3 (January 1965), 254–284.

Aspaturian, Vernon V., "Soviet Foreign Policy at the Crossroads: Conflict and/or Collaboration?" *International Organization*, XXIII, 3 (Summer 1969), 589–620.

Bailey, Sydney D., *The Secretariat of the United Nations*, rev. ed. (New York: Frederick A. Praeger, 1964).

Bechhoefer, Bernard G., *Postwar Negotiations for Arms Control* (Washington, D.C.: Brookings Institution, 1961).

Becker, Benjamin M., *Is the United Nations Dead?* (Philadelphia: Whitmore Publishing Co., 1969).

Bloomfield, Lincoln P., *The United Nations and U.S. Foreign Policy*, 2nd ed. (Boston: Little Brown, 1967).

Brinkley, George A., "The Soviet Union and the United Nations: The Changing Role of the Developing Countries," *The Review of Politics*, XXXII, 1 (January 1970), 91–123.

Burns, Arthur Lee, and Nina Heathcote, *Peacekeeping by U.N. Forces: From Suez to the Congo* (New York: Frederick A. Praeger, 1963).

Butler, William E., "The Soviet Union and the Continental Shelf," *American Journal of International Law*, LXIII, 1 (January 1969), 103–107.

Claude, Inis L., Jr., "The United Nations, the United States, and the Maintenance of Peace," *International Organization*, XXIII, 3 (Summer 1969), 621–636.

Coffey, J. I., "The Soviet View of a Disarmed World," *Journal of Conflict Resolution*, VIII, 1 (March 1964), 1–6.

Cox, Arthur M., *Prospects for Peacekeeping* (Washington, D.C.: Brookings Institution, 1967).

Crane, Robert D., "Soviet Attitude Toward International Space Law," *American Journal of International Law*, LVI, 3 (July 1962), 685–723.

Dallin, Alexander, *The Soviet Union at the United Nations* (New York: Frederick A. Praeger, 1962).

Emerson, Rupert, and Inis L. Claude, Jr., "The Soviet Union and the United Nations: An Essay in Interpretation," *International Organization*, VI, 1 (February 1952), 1–26.

Fernbach, Alfred P., *Soviet Coexistence Strategy* (Washington, D.C.: Public Affairs Press, 1960).

Finkelstein, Lawrence S., ed., *The United States and International Organization: The Changing Setting* (Cambridge: The M.I.T. Press, 1969).

———, "Arms Inspection," *International Conciliation*, No. 540, 1962.

Gardner, Richard N., *In Pursuit of World Order: U.S. Foreign Policy and International Organization* (New York: Frederick A. Praeger, 1964).

———, "The Soviet Union and the United Nations," *Law and Contemporary Problems*, XXIX, 4 (Autumn 1964), 845–857.

Ginsburgs, George, "Soviet Atomic Energy Agreements," *International Organization*, XV, 1 (Winter 1961), 49–65.

———, " 'Wars of National Liberation' and the Modern Law of Nations—The Soviet Thesis," *Law and Contemporary Problems*, XXIX, 4 (Autumn 1964), 910–942.

Goodman, Elliot R., "The Cry of National Liberation: Recent Soviet Attitudes Toward National Self-Determination," *International Organization*, XIV, 1 (Winter 1960), 92–106.

Goodrich, Leland M., *Korea: A Study of U.S. Policy in the United Nations* (New York: Harper and Row, Publishers, Inc., 1956).

Gordenker, Leon, *The United Nations and the Peaceful Unification of Korea: The Politics of Field Operations* (The Hague: Martinus Nijhoff, 1959).

Gross, Franz, ed., *The United States and the United Nations* (Norman, Okla.: University of Oklahoma Press, 1964).

Grzybowski, Kazimierz, *Soviet Public International Law: Doctrines and Diplomatic Practice* (Leyden: A. W. Sijthoff, 1970).

Haas, Ernest B., *Tangle of Hopes: American Commitments and World Order* (Englewood Cliffs, N.J.: Prentice-Hall, 1969).

Haviland, H. Field, Jr., "The United States and the United Nations," *International Organization*, XIX, 3 (Summer 1965), 643–665.

Higgins, Benjamin, *The United Nations and United States Foreign Economic Policy* (Homewood, Ill.: Richard D. Irwin, 1962).

Higgins, Rosalyn, *The Development of International Law Through the Political Organs of the United Nations* (London: Oxford University Press, 1963).

————, *Conflict of Interests: International Law in a Divided World* (Chester Springs, Pa.: Dufour Editions, 1965).

————, ed., *United Nations Peacekeeping, 1946–1967: Documents and Commentary.* I: The Middle East; II: Asia (London: Oxford University Press, 1969, 1970).

Hyde, L. K., Jr., *The United States and the United Nations* (New York: Manhattan Publishing Co., 1960).

Jacobson, Harold Karan, *The USSR and the UN's Economic and Social Activities* (Notre Dame: University of Notre Dame Press, 1963).

————, "The Soviet Union, the UN and World Trade," *The Western Political Quarterly*, XI, 3 (September 1958), 673–688.

————, "The USSR and ILO," *International Organization*, XIV, 3 (Summer 1960), 402–428.

James, Alan, *The Politics of Peacekeeping* (New York: Frederick A. Praeger, 1969).

Kay, David A., *The New Nations in the United Nations, 1960–1967* (New York: Columbia University Press, 1970).

Kramish, Arnold, *The Peaceful Atom in Foreign Policy* (New York: Harper and Row, Publishers, Inc., 1963).

Lall, Arthur, *The UN and the Middle East Crisis, 1967* (New York: Columbia University Press, 1968).

Lefever, Ernest W., *Uncertain Mandate: Politics of the U.N. Congo Operation* (Baltimore: The Johns Hopkins Press, 1967).

Lie, Trygve, *In The Cause of Peace* (New York: The Macmillan Company, 1954).

Lissitzyn, Oliver, "International Law in a Divided World," *International Conciliation*, No. 542, 1963.

Masters, Roger, "The Emperor's Old Clothes: Russia and the United Nations," *The Yale Review*, LII, 2 (December 1962), 176–187.

McWhinney, Edward, "Changing International Law Method and Objectives in the Era of the Soviet-Western Détente," *American Journal of International Law*, LIX, 1 (January 1965), 1–15.

————, *International Law and World Revolution* (1967).

Morozov, G., *International Organization: Some Theoretical Problems* (Moscow: Mysl, 1969).

Morozov, G., and E. Pchelintsev, *The United Nations—Twenty Years of Failures and Successes* (Moscow: Novosti Press Agency, 1965).

————, "Behind the U.N. 'Financial Crisis,'" *International Affairs* (Moscow), No. 6 (June 1964), 23–29.

Nicholas, H. G., "The United Nations in Crisis," *International Affairs* (London), XLI, 3 (July 1965), 441–450.

Padelford, Norman J., and Leland M. Goodrich eds., *The United Nations in the Balance: Accomplishments and Prospects* (New York: Frederick A. Praeger, 1965).

Rajan, M. S., *United Nations and Domestic Jurisdiction* (Bombay: Orient Longmans, 1958).

Ramundo, Bernard A., *Peaceful Coexistence: International Law in the Building of Communism* (Baltimore: The Johns Hopkins Press, 1967).

Rosner, Gabriella, *The United Nations Emergency Force* (New York: Columbia University Press, 1963).

Rosser, Richard F., "Soviet Opposition to Racial Discrimination in the United Nations," *The Russian Review*, XXI, 1 (January 1962), 25–37.

Rubinstein, Alvin Z., *The Soviets in International Organizations: Changing Policy Toward Developing Countries, 1953–1963* (Princeton: Princeton University Press, 1964).

——, "The U.S.S.R. and I.M.C.O.: Some Preliminary Observations," U.S. Naval Institute *Proceedings*, LXXXV, 10 (October 1959), 75–79.

——, "Selected Bibliography of Soviet Works on the United Nations, 1946–1959," *American Political Science Review*, LIV, 4 (December 1960), 985–991.

——, "Soviet and American Policies in International Economic Organizations," *International Organization*, XVIII, 1 (Winter 1964), 29–52.

——, "On IAEA's Future," *Bulletin of the Atomic Scientists*, XXI, 1 (January 1965), 25–27.

Russell, Ruth B., *United Nations Experience With Military Forces: Political and Legal Aspects* (Washington, D.C.: Brookings Institution, 1964).

——, *The United Nations and United States Security Policy* (Washington, D.C.: Brookings Institution, 1968).

Scott, William A., and Stephen B. Withey, *The United States and the United Nations: The Public View, 1945–1955* (New York: Manhattan Publishing Co., 1958).

Sewell, James Patrick, *Functionalism and World Politics* (Princeton: Princeton University Press, 1966).

Sharp, Walter R., *The United Nations Economic and Social Council* (New York: Columbia University Press, 1969).

Shkunaev, V. G., *The International Labor Organization: Past and Present* (Moscow: International Relations Publishing House, 1969).

Simsarian, James, "Outer Space Co-Operation in the United Nations," *American Journal of International Law*, LVII, 4 (October 1963), 854–867.

Stoessinger, John C., *The United Nations and the Superpowers,* 2nd ed. (New York: Random House, 1970).

——, and Associates, *Financing the United Nations System* (Washington, D.C.: Brookings Institution, 1964).

Tunkin, G. I., ed., *Contemporary International Law* (Moscow: Progress Publishers, 1969).

Wainhouse, David W., *International Peace Observation: A History and Forecast* (Baltimore: The Johns Hopkins Press, 1966).

Weiler, Lawrence, D., and Anne Patricia Simons, *The United States and the United Nations* (New York: Manhattan Publishing Co., 1967).

Wilcox, Francis O., and H. Field Haviland, Jr., eds., *The United States and the United Nations* (Baltimore: The Johns Hopkins Press, 1961).

Windass, Stanley, "The Vitality of the United Nations," *The Yale Review,* LIII, 2 (June 1964), 481–496.

Zadorozhny, Georgi, *Peaceful Coexistence: Contemporary International Law of Peaceful Coexistence* (Moscow: Progress Publishers, 1968).

INDEX